Four Green Houses...

One Red Hotel

How to use debt and taxes to get rich

Santiago R. T.

IMPORTANT NOTE:

Exoneration of the responsibility from the editor and the writer.

This book offers information that the author considers reliable about the subject matter, but is sold on the assumption that neither he nor the editor give advice on the needs of anyone, nor the investment adviser, nor provide any other legal advice or accountant. Whoever needs specialized help in matters of legal advice, accounting or financial advice, should contract with the services of a competent professional.

This publication contains performance data collected over many periods of time. Past results do not guarantee future returns. In addition, the performance data, as well as the laws and regulations, change over time, so that the status of the information contained in this book may be altered. This book is not written to be the basis of any financial decision, nor to recommend specific advisors, nor to sell or buy titles.

The author and publisher decline all responsibility for the veracity of the information offered in this book, as well as any loss or risk, personal or corporate, derived, directly or indirectly, from the use or application of the contents of this book.

Note:

Many people who are wealthy will now be among the new poor.

¿Why will some rich be the new poor?

There are many reasons. One of them is because many wealthy people measure their wealth in money.

So, ¿what's wrong about it?

That money is no longer money.

¿So what is the new money?

Financial education is the new money. Financial education today is more powerful than a gun or the lashes and shackles of slavery. The lack of financial education enslaves billions of people around the world.

¿What replaced the lashes, the shackles and the guns?

The monetary system.

¿The monetary system? Our money? How can it control people?

The monetary system is designed to keep people poor, not to help them enrich. It was created to keep people working very hard to get money. Money enslaves those who lack financial education because it makes them slaves of a payroll check, a weekly or biweekly payment.

–Robert Kiyosaki, *Second Chance*

The New York Times of September 24, 1971 says:

"In an international seminar of the International Monetary Fund of recognized economists, they could not agree on what money is and how central banks create it."

In a 2002 article entitled *"Who controls the Federal Reserve?"* Victor Thorn wrote:

"In essence, money has become in nothing more than an illusion, an electronic figure or sum on a computer screen."

Welcome to Wonderland:

- A central bank prints a $ 100 bill out of nowhere.
- It costs $ 0.3 to print the ticket.
- It lends that "debt" of $ 100 to the government with interest.
- The government passes the bill to taxpayers in the form of taxes and inflation.
- The government borrows money again.
- The cycle is repeated forever because it is impossible to pay off the debt ... it can only keep borrowing to pay interest.

Even Houdini would be surprised by such an act of prestidigitation.
It is a system designed by bankers, for bankers.

Senator Robert Lafollette: The United States is controlled by only 50 men.

George F. Baker, partner of J.P. Morgan:

That is totally absurd. I know from personal knowledge that the number of people that the United States controls is not greater than 8.

"Wall Street is the owner of the country. It is no longer a government of the people, by the people and for the people, but a government of Wall Street, by Wall Street and for Wall Street. The common people of this country are slaves and the Monopoly is the Master. "

–Mary Ellen Lease, Populist Leader

"The major financial crises are not announced in the newspapers, but are treated as a kind of national security secret, so that various rescues and market manipulation activities can be carried out behind the scenes."

–John Hoefle

"In the central bank, if you need money for anything, you just need to sit down, write down some figures on the computer and, through a click, assign them to someone who is willing to do what you are asked to do with them."

–Chris Powell

"Gold is money. Everything else is debt. "

–J. P. Morgan

"Paper money will disappear."

–Elon Musk

Q: What would you do if you were still the President of the Federal Reserve?

Alan Greenspan: Resign myself.

"The dollar standard has inherent flaws and it is increasingly unstable. Its death is imminent. "

–Richard Duncan

These are some of the most serious problems facing our world today:

- The collapse of the dollar.
- The increase in public debt.
- The rise in the price of oil.
- The growth of the gap between the rich and all others.
- The decrease in wages.
- The export of jobs to countries with cheaper labor.
- The retirement of millions of people.
- The disappearance of savings.
- The trade war between China and the United States.
- Lack of financial education in schools.

You still have time to prepare for the financial storms that will come ... but not much time.

If you do not decide to be rich, it is more likely that you will become poor.

Television and movies have conditioned us to wait for some politician or social leader to appear in a heroic act and fix the situation, but the hero never appears, because all the political factions that are in power are controlled by the same banking cartel.

Chapters

Glossary of terms

The best of our blog

About us

Books by the same author

Bibliography

Contact us

Preface

The following conversation was published in the British magazine Punch, on April 3, 1957. I think it is the best way to start this book.

Q: What are banks for?

A: To make money.

Q: For its customers?

A: For banks.

Q: Why does not bank advertising mention this?

A: It would not be in good taste. But it is implicitly mentioned in the reserves of $ 249,000,000 or more. That is the money they have made.

Q: From its customers?

A: I guess so.

Q: They mention assets for $ 500,000,000 or more. They have done that too?

A: Not exactly. That is the money they use to make money.

Q: I see. And they keep it in a hidden safe?

A: Not at all. They lend it to customers.

Q: So they do not have it?

A: No.

Q: So how are they active?

A: They argue that they are active if they manage to get that money back.

Q: But they should have some money in a safe somewhere, right?

A: Yes, normally $ 500,000,000 or more. This money is considered a liability.

Q: But if they do, how can it be considered a liability?

A: Because it is not theirs.

Q: Then why do they have it?

A: It has been lent by the clients.

Q: You mean that customers lend money to the bank?

A: Indeed. They put money into their accounts, so it really lends to banks.

Q: And what do banks do with that money?

A: They lend it to other clients.

Q: But did not you say that the money that is lent to other people is considered an asset?

A: Yes.

Q: So assets and liabilities are the same thing?

A: You really cannot say that.

Q: But you just said it. If I put $ 100 in my account, the bank has an obligation to pay it back, so it is a liability. But they go and lend it to someone else, and that person must pay them back, so it is an asset. They are the same $ 100, right?

A: Yes. But…

Q: Then it's canceled. Does it mean, if I'm not wrong, that banks really do not have any money?

A: Theoretically...

Q: It does not matter if it is theoretically. And if they do not have any money, where do they get their reserves of $ 249,000,000 or more?

A: I already told you. That is the money they have made.

Q: How?

A: Well, when you lend your $ 100 to someone else, they charge you interest.

Q: How much?

A: It depends on the bank rate. Let's say 5.5%. That is your gain.

Q: Why is not that my gain? Is not that my money?

A: It is the theory of banking practice that...

Q: When I lend you my $ 100, why do not I charge you interest?

A: You do it.

Q: Do not tell me. How much?

A: It depends on the bank's rates. Let's say 0.5%.

Q: Is it a joke?

A: But only if you are not going to withdraw your money again.

Q: But of course I'm going to withdraw my money again. If I did not want to take it out again I would have buried it in my garden

A: They would not like you to take it out again.

Q: Why not? If I keep it there you say it's a liability to them. Would not you be grateful that you reduce your liabilities by removing that money?

A: No, because if you remove it, you cannot lend it to anyone else.

Q: But if I want to take them out they have to leave me, right?

A: Certainly.

Q: But suppose they have already lent it to another client. What would happen?

A: Then they will give you someone else's money.

Q: But let's suppose that person also wants to take out their money and that they have already given it to me...?

A: You're being foolish by the way.

Q: I think I'm deciphering this. What would happen if everyone wanted their money back at the same time?

A: It is the theory of banking practice that says that will never happen.

Q: So the theory of banks is based on the fact that they do not have to fulfill their commitments?

A: I would not say that.

P: Naturally. Well, if you do not think there is something else you have to tell me...

A: Much more. Now you can go and open an account in the bank.

Q: Only one last question.

A: Of course.

Q: Would not it be better to open a bank myself?

All presidents are just an appearance to distract you from the people who truly control the game.

Please understand:

It does not matter who the president is.

It does not matter who is in the congress.

It does not matter if the system is socialist or capitalist.

It does not matter if the Democrats or the Republicans win.

In the end, the rich will become richer, the poor poorer and the middle class will work harder.

It has always been this way throughout history and will continue in the same way.

Everything has already been tried.

There have been capitalist countries.

There have been socialist countries.

There have been all kinds of leaders and all kinds of ideologies.

The result is always the same: the richest 1% controls all the others through the hidden global financial system ... a system that goes beyond the reach of all presidents and political leaders.

If you think the government will serve you and take care of your problems, then you also believe in Santa Claus.

I hate to be the one who has to tell you this, but the world does not work as you think.

Keep reading, and let me show you the global Monopoly board.

FIRST PART

The Elite's Game

"Through a network of anonymous financial webs, only a handful of world bankers kings own and control everything. Everyone, people, companies, state and foreign countries, have all become slaves tied to the credit ropes of bankers. "

–Hans Schicht, The Death of Banking

Today, no currency in the world is backed by gold or silver.

Today, there is no difference between debt and money.

Today, there is nothing that really limits the amount of debt that can be created.

Today, both governments and citizens are indebted to bankers ... indebted for money they created on a computer screen.

Today, we are experiencing the biggest credit bubble in history. If it continues to expand it can cause hyperinflation. If it bursts it can cause a depression like the one of 1929.

Today, the central banks of the G7 are conspiring in synchrony to keep the system artificially standing.

Today, banks hold hostage the economy as a whole.

Nowadays, governments and their respective central banks are devaluing their currencies on purpose to boost exports, turning savers into losers.

Today, the richest people in the world bet on Wall Street ... with taxpayers' money.

Nowadays, ordinary people have no idea what is happening.

Nowadays, people really believe that the solution to the problems will be when a new puppet is put in Washington.

Nowadays, people continue leaving the university without any financial education.

We currently live in a world in which the growth of debt drives economic growth, therefore, the economy as a whole is a hostage of the banking sector.

Let's begin to walk the long road that lies ahead to discover why, at present, a group of bankers has entangled us in a web of debts that can never be paid.

Chapter 1
The bankers

Question: What is the difference between a banker and Jesse James?

Answer: Jesse James robbed banks from abroad and bankers steal them from the inside.

Question: What is the best way to rob a bank?

Answer: The best way to steal a bank is to have one.

–William Crawford

The subtitle of this book is *"how to use debt and taxes to get rich"*. It is sensible, therefore, to know the rules of the game before trying to win it. These rules are imposed by two very important players: bankers and politicians. In the following chapters we will analyze how the relationship of both has evolved throughout history to reach the present, and how this relationship affects our lives every day.

Money is a very complex issue for most people, especially because what people call money is not really money, but debt. In the following pages you will discover something incredible: the money you have in your wallet does not really belong to you. It is a promissory note that printed a private corporation. It is debt. Sooner or later, that money will go to where it came from: a bank. But let's not get ahead. Let's start at the beginning. It all started thousands of years ago...

Humanity has been advancing throughout its history, and money has also been advancing at the same time. As life has become more sophisticated and modern, the need for more efficient means of conducting business transactions has grown. This has caused the money to evolve and the concept we have of it. Next, I will show you the types of money that have existed throughout history.

Commodity money: This was the first type of money with exact measurement that existed in the history of mankind. The people agreed to give value to some tangible objects and began to trade with them. Instead of exchanging chickens for goats, as they previously did in the "barter" system, people began using commodities with more accurate value measures, such as gold and silver. This was a simpler way of doing transactions, since it demanded much less time and provided greater security to both parties: sellers and buyers.

At present, gold and silver are still products accepted throughout the world as money. In fact, they are the only products that have been a safeguard for people in times of crisis throughout history.

Receipt money: In ancient times, when merchants wished to travel to distant lands, they had to transport their gold or silver with them. This was very dangerous because those trips were long and on the way they could meet thieves who would strip them of everything.

To protect their precious metals, people began to give them to someone they trusted to keep in a vault and gave them a "receipt" for the amount of gold or silver they had deposited. This phenomenon gave rise to banking. When money ceased to be a tangible object such as gold or silver, and became a derivative of these metals, as were receipts, businesses began to take off and transactions became more comfortable and quickly. The merchants could now undertake their long business trips without having to carry precious metals with them. Instead, they carried receipts from bankers that represented a certain value in gold or silver. If the merchants wanted to buy something, they simply used the receipts and these were accepted as money, since they could be exchanged in their entirety for a specific amount of gold or silver that was well stored in a vault. Once a seller accepted a receipt as payment, he deposited it in his own bank and the two banks involved (the buyer's and the seller's) took stock and reconciled the exchange accounts between the buyer and the seller with the debits, and the credits against the receipts. The monetary system began to take shape and modern banking was taking its first steps to reach the system that we have today.

Nowadays, people believe that the money they have is "receipt money", that is, they believe that the value of the paper money they have is backed by a precious metal such as gold or silver, and that these are stored in the vault of some bank. However, as we will see later, it does not work that way. The jump that gave the money then changed the world more than the iPhone or YouTube.

Fractional Reserve Money: The bankers realized something amazing: people rarely returned to them to change their receipts for gold or silver. People preferred the receipts, since they were more comfortable. So the bankers began to have dangerous ideas: "It is a pity to have all this amount of gold and silver in our vaults without doing anything. Every day people come asking for loans and they are very desperate to get a little money. Nobody ever comes to claim those precious metals and everything is very boring around here. Why do not we print some receipts, loans and make a profit? Let's put that money to work instead of leaving it in the vault, accumulating dust". Bankers have learned from experience that very few depositors want to recover their gold at the same time. Depositors who want their gold back never exceed 10 or 15% of the reserves. The bankers consider that it is perfectly safe to lend up to 85% of their gold to anyone who accepts it and is willing to pay interest to use it for a certain time.

In this way, people who were solely in charge of safeguarding the precious metals of their clients, now had become lenders. The bankers had stopped accumulating wealth, and now they were dedicating themselves to "lending" it, in order to earn more money. At first, they did not share the interest they earned with their depositors. It was not until after many years that depositors began to receive an interest from bankers. However, at first, they had no idea that the gold and silver stored in a vault had been lent to someone else.

IT IS A FRAUD TO "LENT" DEPOSITS

Regardless of whether or not depositors receive a portion of the bank's profits from using their money and lending it with interest, we must consider whether those deposits could be "lent" in the first place. Suppose we are going to play a game of poker at Steve's house. Each of us gives $ 30 to Steve, who, acting like a banker, puts all our money in a box and gives us, in exchange for the money, 30 poker chips each. If we want to go home and stop playing, we can exchange each chip for $ 1 that Steve owns. Now suppose that Steve's brother, Howard, appears, not to play poker with all of us, but to borrow some money from Steve. As in total we are playing five people, Steve has in his power $ 150, just the amount his brother needs. You can get the idea of what would happen if Steve decided to lend that money. Neither Steve nor any of the players present has the right to lend that money, since he is in trust, that is, he is fulfilling a contract that Steve has with his guests. That money technically no longer exists as money, but its monetary value has been replaced by poker chips. If Howard manages to convince us of his story and we decide to lend him the money all, we have to lend him a different money than Steve has saved or exchange our poker chips for that money and then lend it to Howard. In the latter case, of course, we could not continue playing. *We cannot spend or lend the deposit we made for $ 150 and then continue playing poker believing that those poker chips have some value.* It is something basic. For example, if you have an apartment in a residential complex and you cannot attend an important assembly where you are going to vote on administrative matters, you can give your vote to someone else who is a member if you cannot present yourself to the assembly. But you cannot appear after the person who replaced you voted for you with the intention to vote as well. In the same way, at the beginning of the banking, the receipts that the bankers gave in exchange for the gold they had in their vaults were representatives of the same. Therefore, that gold that was saved could not be loaned to anyone else unless the person who had the original receipt returned it first. While the person who made the deposit of the gold has the receipt, the monetary value of the gold has been assigned to said receipt. It's simple common sense. Let me give you a small example to better understand this.

Let's Suppose I go to a banker to deposit gold. In return, he gives me a receipt for $ 100,000, that is, for the amount of gold I deposit. The banker now has gold in his vault for $ 100,000, while I have a receipt that can be used as money to buy products or that I can also use to recover all of my gold whenever I want. Everything is going quite well so far.

A few days pass and an entrepreneur appears at the bank that needs capital to finance his business. The banker writes a receipt for $ 100,000 at 10% interest, which is just the amount the entrepreneur needs, who is now happy because he will be able to boost his new business. The banker has just committed fraud and, if we adhere to the laws that govern us, I should go to jail. Of course, what is illegal for us is legal for banks. Let's review what is happening so far:

1. The banker has $ 100,000 in gold coins that I deposit.

2. For that deposit I got a receipt of $ 100,000, which I can now spend at my whim in the economy or I can use to get my gold back when I want it.

3. An employer accepts a receipt of $ 100,000 from the bank, which can be used to claim gold at that bank for the same

amount, even though that person did not deposit any amount of gold to receive the receipt in the first place.

4. The bank now has $ 200,000 in receipts against a $ 100,000 gold reserve. In this case, the fractional reserve is 50% or 1 to 2: the bank prints $ 2 in receipts for each gold coin it holds. The bank has just created money out of nowhere. The magic show started and the bank started taking money out of an empty hat.

5. There is now $ 200,000 in the economy against a $ 100,000 gold reserve. If the people who own that $ 200,000 go to the bank to exchange their gold receipts at the same time, they will realize that everything is an act of magic and that the bank does not have enough gold. This phenomenon is known as "bank panic". When this happened in antiquity, the bank declared bankruptcy for being insolvent and was forced to close its doors. Savers became losers.

The previous example is simple logic. Imagine that I rent a house to five people at the same time and then I pocketed the money. Obviously, it would not be long before I was imprisoned for fraud. However, the bankers had devised a very similar scam by creating a system in which they negotiate, not things of value, but paper receipts that supposedly represent something of value that is stored in some vault. It is a top-level Ponzi scheme. Even today, people believe that the bank lends money to its depositors. It just does not work like that. Depositors have never dared to question how banks can lend their money and still have it on hand to return it when requested. If the bank lent your money, how is it that you have it on your card? Why can you still make purchases with that money? Is not it supposed to be lent to someone else? Why can the bank return it to you whenever you want if someone else is supposed to be using it? How is it that the masses are so naive and never question anything?

We must also address another issue, which is about the honesty and the ability of banks to fulfill their contracts. When the bank uses the gold it has in reserve as the basis for creating new money in the form of loans, the bank is putting itself in a position where it will not have enough gold in its vaults to fulfill its contracts in case depositors want to take the gold to their homes. In other words, the loan contracts were made with full knowledge that, if certain circumstances exist, the banks would be bankrupt. Of course, banks will never talk about this. I will put it to you in the following way: *banks are the only ones that can sign contracts that they know in advance that they cannot comply.* If you or I did something like that, we would go to prison for fraud.

THE FRACTIONAL RESERVE BANKING SYSTEM

Things started to get complicated when banks started doing magic tricks. The banks granted receipts to all those who made gold deposits. If a total of $ 1,000,000 in gold was deposited, the bank delivered receipts for that same amount to the depositors. As we saw earlier, these receipts are money that people can use to buy products and services in the economy. Everything was fine. While the money supply was conformed by "money of receipt", there was no problem and bank panics did not exist. But with the fractional reserve system, the bank now lent a multiple of its deposits. This meant that they were artificially expanding the money supply, causing inflation and devaluing the receipts they printed. At this point, the receipts were no longer 100% backed by gold. They were only backed by the reserve percentage, say, 10%. That means that if you got a receipt for depositing $ 100,000 in gold, now that $ 100,000 receipt was only backed by the gold equivalent of $ 10,000. Very quietly and without calling your attention, the bank had stolen. Today the exact same thing happens, but in a much more sophisticated way.

Despite this silent robbery of people's wealth and the artificial expansion of the money supply that destabilized the economy and caused inflation, the receipts granted by the banks remained valid, although the gold behind them now only represented a fraction of the its value. The money was no longer "cash of receipt" but "fractional reserve money". This process continues today in practically the whole world and is carried out under the name of "fractional reserve system". Although today the rules have changed a bit. In antiquity, the reserve that the banks spoke of was gold or silver. Nowadays, the so-called "reserves" are only government bonds or debt instruments. That is, the global economic system today has no support for any precious metal, but the entire world economy is supported by promissory notes that represent the government's promise to pay off the debt with their respective interests. You can imagine who really pays this debt: the taxpayers. We'll talk about this later in another chapter.

Bankers in ancient times never bothered to explain the dark secret of what they did. The fractional reserve system became a well-kept secret of the profession. The depositors were too naive, even today, and preferred not to ask how the banks lent their money to someone else but still have it available to return when requested.

Let's take a step backwards for a moment and analyze what we've been up to now.

Commodity → Receipt → Fractional Res. System

1. At first, the bankers provided the service of keeping the precious metals of the people and, in return, they delivered a receipt equivalent to the amount of gold or silver deposited. This receipt was used to buy products and services in the economy, or it could be used to recover deposits made at any time. At this point, the "commodity money" became "receipt money". This was a great advance and I made the transactions more easily and in a faster way. However, this does not alter the money supply. If a bank had $ 1,000,000 in gold in its vaults, there were receipts worth $ 1,000,000 in the economy. The entire money supply was backed by all the gold or silver in the bank's vault. Bank panics did not exist and people's savings were safe. People have never heard the term "inflation" or

"deflation" at this point. People could either use their gold coins or use the receipt issued by the bank for storing these coins, but they could not use both. If they used the gold, the receipt was not issued. If they used the receipt, the gold was kept in the vault and was not in circulation.

2. Over time, the bankers decided to abandon this practice by implementing the fractional reserve system and became magicians when they began issuing receipts from nowhere and lending them to the public. Technically, it is wrong to say that they were creating money out of nowhere. It is not entirely true. While it is true that there was no precious metal that backed all of that newly issued money, if there was anything behind it. The bankers began to back their receipts with debt. We'll talk about this debt monetization later, but for the moment, you should only understand the following: the fractional reserve system allows the bank to create new money only if someone borrows it. Under this system, if nobody borrows money, the money supply remains constant, so in general, there is no inflation.

HOW DEBT IS CREATED THROUGH THE FRACTIONAL RESERVE BANKING SYSTEM

Before moving on to the next type of money, it is important to know how the printing presses of banks work thanks to the fractional reserve system.

The banks accept deposits. These deposits serve two purposes: to have reserves and to lend. As we have seen, banks have reserves to guarantee that they have liquidity to be able to deal with customers who want to withdraw their money. If they did not do this, the result would be a bank panic and bank bankruptcy. In ancient times, banks were required to hold those reserves in the form of gold or silver. Today it is not necessary for a bank to have gold and silver and, sometimes, some banks can operate without having any reserves. A fractional reserve banking system is one in which banks do not have 100% reserves to deal with their deposits. In this type of system, banks create deposits by lending a pre-established multiple of the reserves they have. I'll give you an example.

Let`s suppose that the following banks must have a fractional reserve of gold equivalent to 20% of their deposits. The process begins when Bank A accepts a gold deposit worth $ 100. To comply with the obligation to have 20% reserves, classify $ 20 in gold as a reserve and the remaining $ 80 is classified as "excess reserves". Excess reserves can be loaned to someone else. The person who borrows the $ 80 deposits them later in his bank, the Bank B. The Bank B sets aside 20% of the $ 80 for reserves, that is, gold valued at $ 16. The remaining $ 64 is lent, and ends up stopping at Bank C.

This process is repeated several more rounds, until it reaches zero. The final result is revealing: an initial deposit of gold worth $ 100 ends up leaving in the banking system $ 500 of deposits and $ 400 of debt in an act of prestidigitation known by the name of Fractional Reservation Banking System. To comply with the reserve obligation, an amount equivalent to the initial deposit is set aside, that is, $ 100. Let me show you how it works:

	Deposits	**Reserve**	**Loans**
Round 1	100	20	80
Round 2	80	16	64
Round 3	64	12.8	51.2
Round 4	51.2	10.24	40.96
Round 5	40.96	8.192	32.768
Round 6	32.768	6.5536	26.2144
Round 7	26.2144	5.24	20.97
Round 8	20.97	4.19	16.77
Round 9	16.77	3.354	13.416
Round 10	13.416	2.68	10.73
Round 11	10.73	2.146	8.58
Round 12	8.58	2	6.86
Round 30	0,2	0	0,1
Round 31	0,1	0	0,1
Total	**500**	**100**	**400**

(Note: The numbers are approximate and not all decimals are included, the purpose of this example is to illustrate how the fractional reservation system works.

Like the trick of a magician, it is necessary to look at it several times before understanding that it is only an act of prestidigitation. As can be seen, the fractional reserve banking system creates debt and deposits. In the previous example, a debt of $ 400 was created using $ 100 as a reserve. It is important to keep in mind that the reserve ratio is the factor that determines the maximum amount of deposits (and, therefore, debt) that can be created. In this example, at the end of the entire process, there are $ 500 of deposits, that is, five times more than the amount of gold deposited initially, and $ 400 of credit that did not exist before. In this case, the money multiplier is 5, which means that for every dollar deposited in the bank, it could lend $ 5. If the reserve coefficient had been 10% only, the money multiplier would have been 10 and the banking system would have ended up having $ 1,000 of deposits, that is, 10 times the amount of gold deposited initially, and therefore, $ 900 again credit.

Check very carefully the previous picture and its meanings. If it costs you a bit to understand, get together with a friend and discuss it. The most likely thing is that the smarter and more honest you are, the less you will find the previous painting. I bet you will not find a scam greater than the one I just showed you. All of the above is nothing more than an act of prestidigitation and, like a magic trick, depends on deception to make it work.

From the moment that the bankers discovered that they could lend a multiple of the money they really had, the money supply began to expand based on the reserve of gold that the banks had in their deposits. The problem is that, throughout history, the reserve that banks have is getting smaller and smaller ... until it reaches zero. Once a bank has no obligation to have gold in its vaults or any precious metal, money ceases to be money and becomes a simple *Fiat* currency, or money by decree.

Fiat Money: As bankers get a lot of interest from the fractional reserve money loans they make, the temptation to create as much as they want is very high. As this happens, the fraction representing the reserve becomes smaller and smaller until one day, eventually, it is reduced to zero and becomes pure Fiat money. This is the money we have today. Money, as we know it, has already started its long journey where it has degenerated more and more, until it becomes mere paper money, or Fiat money. Fiat money is paper money by government decree, which is not backed by gold or silver. Technically, it does not have any kind of value. These are its main characteristics:

1. It does not represent anything of intrinsic value.

2. It is money by decree, which means that there is a law imposed by the government that forces everyone to accept it as a currency to trade.

These two characteristics always go together, since as the Fiat money really is not worth anything, the public would soon reject it and adopt a more reliable means of exchange, such as gold or silver. Therefore, when governments and central banks issue Fiat money, they do so under a law that threatens fines and imprisonment for those who refuse to use it. The only way a piece of paper can be exchanged by a government in exchange for goods and services that have tangible value is to give citizens no other option than to accept the newly printed monopoly money.

At this point, it is essential to clarify something: Fiat money is not money really. The correct term to refer to this is "Fiat currency". All the "monies" we saw earlier (commodity, receipt, fractional reserve) were really money because they were backed by something of value. Even fractional reserve money is money (assuming that the so-called "reserve" is gold or silver), since, although it is not fully backed, it has something of value. The problem is that many believe that currency is money, and that is why people work hard for it and then save it, thinking that they are treasuring something valuable. They cannot be more wrong. A Fiat currency, or currency by decree, is technically worthless. The only thing that has as support is "the good faith and the credit of the government". Money, unlike currency, has value in itself. Nowadays, the harsh reality is that money does not exist: there are only currencies. All currencies in use in practically all developed countries are Fiat currencies. The fact that the whole world has abandoned gold and silver as a backing for money is the main reason for the current global financial crisis and the credit bubble that has grown exponentially in recent decades.

Once banks abandoned the discipline that gold demanded, there were no limits to the amount of money they could print.

There is a dark secret that no politician will mention while campaigning: the Fiat currencies are designed to lose their value. In fact, since they really are not worth anything, sooner or later they end up returning to their original value: zero. The only purpose of a Fiat currency is to confiscate the wealth of the people and transfer it to the government and the banks. Every time the government prints a new dollar through its central bank and spends it, or whenever a commercial bank makes a loan with money newly created for that purpose, they keep all the purchasing power of that new money.

Where does the purchasing power come from? It was stolen from your money in secret. Each time a new dollar comes into circulation in the economy, it devalues all other existing dollars, because now there are more dollars to acquire the same amount of goods and services. It is supply and demand; basic economy inflating the money supply in this way causes the prices of products and assets to increase. The above is the description of the most deceitful and hidden tax that exists, and probably already know: inflation. Inflation takes over your wealth and strips you piecemeal. Fiat money is the main cause of inflation, and the amount that people lose purchasing power is exactly the amount that was taken from them and transferred to their government and banks through this process. Inflation is the most unjust tax of all because it falls more heavily on those who are unable to pay it: wage earners and those who have a fixed income. It also specializes in severely punishing savers by devaluing the value of their savings each year.

THE COLLAPSE OF THE GREAT EMPIRES

During the last 2,400 years, a pattern has been repeated continuously: governments have ended up replacing the "commodity money" with "Fiat money" and, in this way, have ended up destroying the economy and the civilization that had prospered so much. By studying the great civilizations that have preceded us, one can easily visualize how they have gone from glory to misery.

1. An empire begins its development by implementing receipt money, which gives the people the security of trading knowing that in some vault there is a quantity of gold and silver equivalent to the amount of paper money that is in circulation in the economy. Inflation is practically zero since no bank or government is artificially inflating the money supply by creating more money out of nowhere. The town prospers enormously.

2. As the empire develops economically and socially, the economic commitments begin to grow, which increases the social programs and spending on public works.

3. The empire realizes that now it has many riches and enjoys a lot of prosperity, so that politics begins to become more influential and therefore begins to allocate a significant amount of money to the financing of the army and its respective weapons. In this way, it seeks to protect the empire from possible attacks, or even invade nearby empires and expand to grow more economically.

4. At some point, the army enters into operation, either by an attack by an external force or by a campaign of invasion to other lands. This generates that the expenses overflow.

5. The government, once facing the war, the greatest expense of all, has no other choice: it must steal the wealth of its people, and this is achieved silently replacing the money that worked until then with a Fiat currency that can be produced in unlimited amounts, because you do not need to have any gold

or silver backing. By implementing a Fiat currency that they can manipulate at will, they can finance all war expenses without having to raise taxes directly, which would be political suicide.

6. Finally, when inflation is triggered in the economy as a result of the large amount of foreign currency that was created for the war, the currency loses all credibility, the system collapses and there is a huge transfer of wealth.

7. Wealth *resembles energy in the following: it never destroys itself, it only transforms*. Wealth is not destroyed in a depression, a bubble, a market collapse or a currency crisis. Simply, it is transferred from the hands of some people, to the hands of other people. Those who realized that the government could not simply print money forever without destroying the currency itself, preferred to exchange their currency for assets that really had a tangible value: real estate for rent, gold and silver. The people who clung to their Fiat currencies ended up transferring all their wealth to the people who acquired real assets instead of saving.

The above is not an isolated case. It has happened innumerable times in history. In fact, it is happening now. The United States is in point five. You have not experienced high inflation for several reasons, but perhaps the most important is that your currency has the status of a world reserve currency. If this hegemony of the dollar were to end, it is likely that tomorrow the dollar would fall. A week later, the rest of the world economy would collapse. We will talk about this later.

The history of great civilizations shows us the following: *a nation that implements Fiat money in its economy has been condemned to misery and political disunity.* No Fiat currency has survived throughout its history. All end, sooner or later, returning to its original value, which is zero.

With the knowledge of what money has been in different parts of history and how bankers have evolved the methods they use, the time has come to travel back in time and study the creation of the first Central Bank in the world: the Bank of England. A warning before continuing: things will get darker and darker. Learning about central and commercial banks is exciting, like reading a good fiction novel. Although there is bad news: even the smallest detail of what you will read below is true.

Let's start going to the exact moment when the game of Monopoly of the elite began, with the creation of the Bank of England, in 1694.

SUMMARY

- When gold or silver was used as money, either through "commodity money" or "receipt money," the government and the banks could not artificially expand the money supply and cause inflation or deflation in the economy.

- With the absence of the gold standard, there is no way to protect savers from the theft of their purchasing power through inflation.

- The fractional reserve money is paper money that is backed by precious metals for only a portion of the total amount. It's a kind of hybrid: a part money receipt, and another part Fiat money. The public ignore this and believes that fractional reserve money can be redeemed for gold or silver in full at any time. Eventually, the truth of this money is discovered, sooner or later. When it happens, there are banking panics and only the first depositors who request their money back are able to recover it. The others realize the harsh reality: the bank all this time was broken and never was able to honor their contracts.

- The bankers do not lend the money they have in deposit, but money recently issued for that purpose through the mechanism called "Fractional Reserve System".

- The Fiat money is paper currency that does not have any endorsement of any precious metal and which, by order of the government, should be used by all people. This type of money benefits the bankers since they can take out of an empty hat the entire amount they want and collect interest. It also benefits politicians, since it allows them to increase spending without having to raise taxes directly. Fiat money is the main cause of inflation, the most unjust hidden tax of all, which falls mainly on those who work for money and then save it.

- Currently, money does not exist; there are only Fiat currencies.

- Fiat money and fractional reserve money are the root of all modern evils in our world. If governments and banks could not print money at will, inflation would disappear almost completely and most modern wars would not have happened since, with a classic gold standard, financing them would mean the economic ruin of a nation.

- Throughout history, whenever a nation has abandoned gold and implemented a Fiat currency, it has been condemned to economic hardship.

Chapter 2
The conspiracy of Jekyll Island

"Let me issue and control the money of a nation and I do not care who writes the laws"

–Mayer Amschel Rothschild

The transition from fractional reserve money to Fiat money requires the government to participate through a dark mechanism called the *central bank*. That's what this chapter will be about. Before starting, we must clarify something: *the central bank of a country is much more powerful than the government itself.*

THE BANK OF ENGLAND

England was going through great economic hardship after more than half a century of wars against France and numerous civil wars, caused by the very high taxes that citizens had to pay. Unable to raise taxes and unable to borrow money for the heavy debts he had, the English parliament was desperately looking for some other way to get money to pay for the expenses he had. The goal was to get money without having to confiscate it directly from people in the form of taxes and without incurring heavy debts with foreign lenders.

There were two groups that saw a unique opportunity because of this new need: politicians, who needed a way to spend all the money they wanted without having to raise taxes directly, and bankers, who could escape the discipline that imposed the gold and had the blessing of the government, could print all the money they wanted out of nowhere and lend it to the public and the government with interests.

The two groups decided to join to form a society and thus join forces to achieve their common goal. More than a society, it really was a conspiracy: they wanted to have the power to manipulate the money supply at will to fulfill their private interests. At a secret meeting in a chapel in London, the newly formed society met to discuss their seven-point plan that would help them achieve their mutual interests:

1. The government would grant the power to form a central bank to the bankers.
2. The bank would have the power to issue "Bank Notes" that would circulate through the economy of England as paper money.
3. The bank could create money out of nowhere and would only be required to have a fraction of the total of its backed currencies.
4. The bank would lend the government all the money it needs.
5. The loans that would be made to the government would be supported mainly by government bonds or promissory notes.
6. Although this money would be created from nowhere and it would not cost the bank anything to create it, the

government would commit to paying an interest to use it, at a rate of 6-8%.

7. Government bonds would be considered "reserves" that would be used as a basis to create additional money, which would be lent to the general public. These loans, of course, would also have interests. This would mean that bankers would collect interest twice for the same nothing.

The circular that was distributed to attract people interested in the initial offer of shares of the bank said the following: *"The Bank gets the interest of all the money that, the Bank, I think of nothing"*. This circular was issued in 1694, and thus the first central bank in the world came to life.

The banking system of "fractional reserve" was formalized with the constitution of the Bank of England, in 1694, and it is a system that exists today and that is used in most of the world. This system, which we analyzed in the previous chapter and will analyze more thoroughly in the next one, involves credits issued by private bankers, which apparently are backed by "reserves". In the beginning, these reserves consisted of gold or even silver, but today they are nothing more than government securities (promises to pay) and any other debt instrument. The banking system often lends these titles, which in essence is called "falsify". The creation of the Bank of England and the functions that fulfilled the blessing of the government marked a before and after in the history of banking.

Both groups that made up the newly created society in London were very pleased by the monster they had just created. The bankers were going to buy government bonds and they were going to buy them with "Bank Notes" just issued from nowhere for that specific purpose. These Bank Notes - which were already considered money thanks to the approval of the central bank - would be issued and would be borrowed with interest. The government benefited because it could borrow all the money it needed in exchange for a few bonds, and the bankers benefited because they could charge interest for money that they created out of nowhere. Who was paying for both parties? The taxpayers. And they did it by paying the public debt that the government had with the bank and through the hidden tax called inflation.

This was the first official act of the first central bank in the world:

1. The government is seeking £ 500,000 to finance the war.
2. The bank only has £ 720,000 invested.
3. The bank lends £ 1,200,000 to the government, more than double what they needed and 66% more than they initially had.
4. The bank has the privilege of creating at least the same amount of money they have (£ 720,000) in the form of loans to the public.
5. The government of England pays you 8% for the loan.
6. The public pays 9% for the loan.
7. The final result is a gain of £ 160,800, more than 22% of your initial investments of £ 720,000.

This first official act of the Bank of England indicated the path that the central banks of the world continue to follow: under the pretense of buying government bonds, central banks act as hidden money creation machines that can be activated in any way. Moment that politicians or commercial banks want. For politicians, this is a very good news, as they do not have to convince the public to raise taxes or rely on good credit from their treasury to raise funds. They just have to call their friend, the central banker, and do "creative accounting" to have all the money they need. And since no one in the public understands this process, it is politically secure.

THE CHEAT OF THE BANKERS

For the magic trick to work and the cheating to be done correctly, the bankers say they charge interest, but this is completely wrong. They did not really lend any money in the first place, but they created it. The real point you must understand is that, under these circumstances, it is irrelevant to talk about the interest rate that the bank says it charges. When a bank creates money out of nowhere, the true return it gets is not 8%, or 9%, or even 22%. It is an infinite return. When you get something for nothing - which is exactly what the bankers get - the return will always be infinite, since you did not invest any capital in the first place.

You may ask yourself: Why does the government of England did not create the money personally, instead of borrowing it with interest? The answer is that, if the government had done this directly, the nature of the Fiat currency would have been recognized immediately and probably would not have been accepted as payment for war expenses. Creating the money through the banking system, however, the process becomes impossible to detect for average people. The Bank Notes are almost unrecognizable to the notes that were previously in circulation and that were backed by gold and silver. Precisely for that reason the public falls into the trap. For example, if you take a ticket from the United States today, at the top you will find the phrase *"Federal Reserve Note"* (Nota de la Reserva Federal). Previously, the tickets had the phrase *"Silver Certificate"* (Certificado de Plata). For the average person, this means nothing. However, as we go further in the operation of banking, you will discover that the difference between one ticket and the other is abysmal: the first is debt, the second is money; the first does not belong to you, the second does; the first is worth less every day, the second has intrinsic value; the first is a fraud, the second has been money for many centuries.

The Bank of England introduced the concept of the alliance between politicians and bankers. Politicians would receive money to spend whatever they wanted (created out of nowhere by bankers) without having to raise taxes directly. In exchange for this favor, the bankers would receive a commission for the transaction (which, for purposes of deception, they call "interest") which they would continue to receive in perpetuity. Since everything seemed to be involved in the mysterious rituals of banking, which the common man was not expected to understand, there was practically no opposition to this scheme. It was the perfect business. And if for some reason the Bank got into trouble, the government would give a hand to its partner and rescue it at whatever cost was necessary. This conspiracy is a society. Both politicians and bankers are committed to protecting each other, not out of loyalty or friendship, but for their mutual interests. They know that, if one of the two fails, the other also. Later, when the Bank of England got into trouble because it could not fulfill its contracts, Parliament intervened immediately. The bank, as part of the agreement, was exempt from honoring its contracts and returning the gold. The free market does not apply to these bankers and, unlike all of us, to them if they are given the necessary help to prevent them from falling into bankruptcy or getting into legal problems. Legitimate capitalism, as we know it, does not apply to large banks. This is not an accident or an isolated case. The system was designed in this way.

THE SECRET DEBT THEFT

It is important to clarify the following point: charging interest for lending money is not a fraud, much less makes the lender a thief. Do not misunderstand. But if I sign a piece of paper that has no value and I lend it to you with interest, then I am committing fraud. Let's analyze the following example and you will understand better what I am trying to tell you.

You are going to buy a house where you want to live, and the budget you have is $ 100,000 dollars. After searching in many neighborhoods, one day you're lucky, and you find your dream home that costs just $ 100,000. Of those $ 100,000, $ 30,000 represents the costs of the land, the architects who designed the house, construction permits and sales commissions. While the rest, that is, the other $ 70,000, cover the costs of the construction itself, that is, the materials, the workers, the machinery and the work of the engineer in charge. Suppose you put $ 30,000 down and the remaining $ 70,000 you borrow from the bank. The bank agrees to give you a loan with an annual interest rate of 11% for a period of 30 years. At the end of that time, you will end up paying $ 167,806 in interest. That means that the amount paid to the bankers who lend the money is much more than what is paid to those who provide all the labor and all the materials. Now, it is true that this figure represents the value in time of that money in 30 years, and can be easily justified arguing that the lender, as in this case is the bank, deserves compensation for allowing them to use their capital and give up to this for a while. But all that would be assuming the following: that the lender really has something to renounce, that he has earned that capital, that he has saved it and then lent it to the construction or acquisition of someone else's home. What could you think, however, of a lender who did not earn that money, did not save it, and to be more precise, simply created it out of nowhere? What is the value in time of nothingness? Do you understand now the fraud that is committed every day? While you get up every day to work and break your back trying to save some money so you can invest, the bankers simply turn on the printing press and celebrate with champagne the amazing ignorance in which people live submerged.

Every dollar, euro, peso, Yuan, yen or pound that exists today in the world, whether in the form of paper money, accounting entry or credit, exists only because someone applied for a loan on that money. It's possible that it was not you, but someone else did it. The meaning of that is that every bill in the world is earning compound interest every day for the banker's kings who created them out of nowhere. What have the bankers done to deserve this cash flow that they earned in perpetuity? Are they lending the money they have earned thanks to their successful investments or the capital obtained through their shareholders? Or do they lend the money saved by the depositors? Unfortunately, no. None of the above is the correct answer. The bankers, even though it does not make much sense, simply wave a magic wand called "Fiat money", and the magic show begins.

THE FRAUD OF CREDIT CARDS

In the case of credit cards and other debts issued by commercial banks today, banks are not lending their own money or that of their depositors. They are lending the borrower's credit, that is, they are transforming the borrower's promise of payment into money. That is confirmed by the Federal Reserve itself, which we will talk about shortly, in *Modern Money Mechanics*, where they say the following:

"Of course, banks do not really grant the loans of the money they receive as deposits. If they did, you could not create additional money. What they do when they give loans, is to accept promissory notes in exchange for credits to the lender's transaction accounts. The loans, which are assets, and the deposits, which are liabilities, are increased by the same amount, keeping the books balanced. "

When you sign a credit card payment receipt at a merchant location, you are creating what is called a "negotiable instrument." A negotiable instrument is a signed document that can be converted into money or used as money. The commercial establishment takes this negotiable instrument that it obtained and deposits it in a special mercantile account required for all those premises that accept credit. The account increases your balance by the value of the payment receipt, indicating that the store has been paid for. The receipt is then sent to the credit card company (VISA, MasterCard, etc.), which collects all your debts and sends them to the bank. The bank then sends you an extract that you pay with a check, causing your account to be debited.

Possibly you noticed the following: at no time the bank has lent your money or that of its depositors. Instead, your payment receipt - or as the bank calls it, a "negotiable instrument" - has become an "asset" against which credit has been granted. The bank has not done anything except monetize your promissory note or the promise that you will pay your debt.

When we lend someone our money, our assets decrease for the same value as the borrower's assets increase. But when a bank lends money to someone else, the bank's assets increase. Their liabilities also increase, since their deposits are accounted as liabilities; but the money is not really there. It is simply an obligation, that is, something that should be paid to the depositor. The bank converts its promise of payment, or "negotiable instrument", into an asset (loan) and a liability (deposit) at the same time, thus balancing its books, while no pre-existing money has been transferred to the borrower's account.

Bank loans, whether by credit cards, mortgages, free investment or whatever, are effectively frauds against the borrowers, since they are paying high interest rates for using something that the lenders never really had. The next chapter will deal mainly with this magic show and the way debt has become all the money today. But before, it is important to know the main magician of this show: The Federal Reserve.

THE FEDERAL RESERVE

Before we start, let us answer the following question: What is the Federal Reserve Bank? The answer will surprise you. Although it hides under the pretense of being the central bank of the United States, the dark reality is that it is not a bank, it has no reserves, and it is not federal. The Fed, as it is popularly known, is a private corporation that pays dividends to its shareholders and acts autonomously. Let's start with a brief look at his birth.

A secret meeting on Jekyll Island in Georgia owned by J. Morgan, in November 1910, it was where the Federal Reserve was born. Organized by Senator Nelson Aldrich, a Morgan partner and John D. Rockefeller's father-in-law, the meeting resulted in the birth of a banking cartel that sought to monopolize the nation's money supply. During the meeting, which lasted several days, six people met, which accounted for almost half of all the wealth in the world at that time. Its objective was clear: to create a central bank to control the world financially and economically.

At the Jekyll Island meeting were the representatives of the most powerful banking consortiums on the planet: Morgan, Rockefeller, Rothschild, Warburg and Kuhn & Loeb. What these consortiums wanted was to intervene in the free market and tilt interest rates downwards, in order to favor debt instead of saving and being able to lend more money created out of nowhere in exchange for interest. To achieve this goal, the economy should abandon the gold standard and Congress should renounce its right to issue the country's money and grant that privilege to the Federal Reserve. These are the challenges that those Magnates faced during the meeting they celebrated:

1. They should devise a way to stop the growth and influence that rival small banks were having, and ensure that control of the country's financial resources did not come out of the hands of attendees who were present at the meeting.

2. How to tilt interest rates downwards so that the money supply becomes more *elastic* and companies start borrowing more frequently. In short, they wanted, little by little, to degrade the fractional reserve money until eventually reaching a system of pure Fiat money.

3. Devise a way to group the reserves of all banks in a large reserve, which would be the central bank that would create, so that the other banks follow the same practices.

4. If this system of low reserves, low interest rates and abundant credits eventually leads to collapse, then they had to make sure that the losses were not borne by the banks but by the taxpayers. The partnership with the government would be key at this point.

5. The most difficult challenge, however, would be to convince Congress to approve this scheme. The banking cartel should devise a way to sell this idea to Congress under the appearance that this bank would be federal, and therefore, would protect the interests of the public and ensure the welfare of the economy as a whole.

Carroll Quigly, mentor to Bill Clinton, wrote about this secret bankers' group the following:

"The objective of the elite of world bankers was to control the world. Its objective was nothing less than to create a global system of financial control in private hands, capable of dominating the political system of each country and the economy of the world as a whole. This system would be feudally controlled by the central banks of the world, acting together through secret agreements. "

The Federal Reserve Act of 1913 approved the Federal Reserve System, after many debates and some changes demanded by Congress. This act gives you the power to issue Federal Reserve notes and put them into circulation in the economy through loans. People had to accept them, trade with them and pay taxes with these tickets. Although this law gave control of the money supply to the Federal Reserve and allowed it to act autonomously, the law required the Fed to have gold reserves of not less than 40% in relation to its Federal Reserve notes circulation. This meant, in a few words, that for every dollar that the Fed issued, it must have gold worth 40 cents. The bankers continued to work and struggle to achieve their ultimate goal: to eliminate gold completely from the equation and to work with Fiat money only. Although it took a few years, they were successful. We will explain this point later.

Congressman Louis McFadden, Chairman of the Banking and Currency Committee of the House of Representatives, on June 10, 1932, referred to the confusion surrounding the Central Bank of the United States:

"Some people think that the Federal Reserve banks are government institutions. They are not. They are private credit monopolies that torment the people of the United States for their personal benefit, that of their foreign and national fraudsters, and that of the rich and predatory lenders. The looting of the United States by the Fed is the greatest crime in history. The Fed has spared no effort to hide its powers, but the truth is that it has usurped the government. Control everything here and control all external relations. Create and destroy governments at will. "

The Fed, therefore, is a private company that does not report to the Government of the United States. It is such a private company that its shares are not even registered in the stock market. None of us can own a fraction of this company. It belongs almost entirely to the most powerful banking consortiums in the world, of which Citibank and J.P. Morgan Chase. These banks represent the financial empires that built J.P. Morgan and John D. Rockefeller, those who, of course, had a strong influence on the creation of the Federal Reserve and its approval by Congress. It consists of twelve regional banks, owned by many commercial banks that hold shares of the Federal Reserve. The Federal Reserve website states the following: *"The Federal Reserve Banks do not operate for profit, and the ownership of a certain number of shares is, by law, a requirement to be a member of the system [...] Dividends are, by law, 6% per annum"* . Translating that into an ordinary language, a company with shares that are privately owned and that offers a guaranteed dividend of 6%, is a private for-profit corporation.

A more precise description to define the Federal Reserve would be simply to say that it is a banking cartel protected by law that has special powers. Something important that must be taken into account, so that there is no confusion, is that the panorama does not change much if the central bank of a country is private or of the government. Even if all the central banks of the world were private, simply turning them into part of the government would not change their main functions. While we would get rid of the bankers who create money for their particular interests, we would instead have the politicians managing the nation's money supply and creating money for political ends. The Bank of England, of which we spoke at the beginning of this chapter, was privately owned in its infancy, but recently it became part of the British government. Its function as central bank remains the same, and nothing substantial has really changed. The same thing happens with the other countries. The central banks of most developed countries belong to their respective governments. Despite this, they do not differ in anything from the Federal Reserve. *Who* owns them is not as important as the *function* they exercise. In addition, as we will see in the next chapter, the ones that really influence the creation of money in a country are private commercial banks.

THE MOST POWERFUL BANKER OF THE WORLD

The director of the Federal Reserve is the most powerful banker on the planet and, unlike the president of the United States, he does not have to worry about reelection every four years and his term is not limited to two periods. The head of the Federal Reserve can be re-elected indefinitely and does not report to anyone. Act in the way you want, whether the president of the day likes it or not. Nathan Rothschild, who controlled the Bank of England after 1820, is quoted as stating the following:

"I do not care that puppet is put on the throne of England to rule the empire in which the sun never sets. The man who controls the British money supply controls the British Empire. And I'm the one who controls the British money supply. "

We depend completely on the banks to survive. Someone has to borrow every dollar we have in circulation for it to exist. If the banks print synthetic money in a massive way, we are prosperous, but if they limit the money-debt, we die of hunger. In the next chapter you will see the whole picture and understand the desperate situation in which the system is. It's almost incredible, but that's how it works. This is the most important issue today that smart people can investigate and reflect on.

We do not own anything that cannot be taken away completely. The real estate market could plummet tomorrow, as could the stock market. The dollar could collapse and also our savings. Even social security and pensions could soon be things of the past. All thanks to the fact that a network of private banks has taken over the creation and control of the world monetary system. An elite of world power intends to obtain absolute control over the planet and its natural resources, including "human capital". The blood of this elite of power is money, and its weapon is fear. Ideology, patriotism, religion and loyalty mean nothing to this banking cartel. Capitalism, communism, socialism, fascism ... it does not care. Any system is fine as long as the money keeps coming. The bankers are the ones who really dominate everything. Politicians come and go, but those who control money remain to choose their successors.

SUMMARY

- The central bank of a country is much more powerful than the government itself.

- In 1694 the first central bank in the world, the Bank of England, was born in London. It was a private corporation that manipulated the money supply at will, paid dividends to its shareholders and gave the government all the credit it needed to fight their wars and cover their expenses.

- The first official act of the new bank created showed its dark pretensions: under the appearance of making a loan, what really was to make money out of nowhere and lend it with interest.

- When a bank creates the money and lends it, its true return is not 5%, or 8%, or 20%. His return is infinite, since it cost him nothing to make that money.

- If the government had created the money directly, the nature of the Fiat currency would have been recognized immediately and probably not accepted. On the contrary, by creating money through the banking system, the process becomes unrecognizable and impossible for average people to detect.

- Every ticket in the world is earning an interest compounded every day by the banker's kings who created them out of nowhere.

- The Federal Reserve, the central bank of the United States, is not a bank, it has no reserves, and it is not federal. The Fed, as it is popularly known, is a private corporation that manipulates the economy, pays dividends to its shareholders and acts autonomously.

- A secret meeting that was held on Jekyll Island in Georgia, in November 1910, was where the Federal Reserve was born. That meeting resulted in the birth of a banking cartel that sought to monopolize the nation's money supply.
- The Federal Reserve Act of 1913 approved the Federal Reserve System. The banking cartel officially became operational in 1914.
- It does not matter a lot if the central bank of a country is a private or government corporation. Even if all the central banks of the world were private, simply turning them into part of the government would not change their main functions.

Chapter 3
Money Heist

"If people understood how our banking and monetary system works, there would be a revolution tomorrow morning."

–Henry Ford

There is a very popular scene in the Netflix series, *"Money Heist"* which is where The Professor - who was the mastermind at the bank - is explained to Rachel - the negotiator by the police - who technically are not doing nothing different from what central banks do on a daily basis. The argument given by the teacher, which is quite convincing, is as follows:

Why do not you want to hear me Rachel? Why am I one of the bad guys? They have taught you to see everything in terms of "good and bad" ... but what we are doing is that it seems good to you if other people do it.

In 2011, the European Central Bank created € 171 billion from scratch, out of the blue! Just like we are doing, in a big way. € 185 billion in 2012. € 145 billion in 2013. Do you know where all that money went? To the banks. Directly from the factory, to the richest. Did someone say that the European Central Bank was a thief? "Liquidity injection", they called it. And they brought him out of nowhere Raquel, out of the blue!

The Professor stands up and looks for a ticket. He takes it, goes back to where Rachel is pointing to the ticket, and says:

What is this? This is nothing Raquel, this is paper (begins to break the ticket). It's paper, see? It is paper. I am doing a "liquidity injection", but not to banking. I am doing it here, in the real economy, of this group of unfortunates who is what we are, Raquel, in order to escape from all this. Do not you want to escape? [...]

Who can argue with so much logic?

The crude truth is that, money does not exist. There are only debts. It is not until someone borrows money and spends it when it comes into circulation in the economy. It is the act of borrowing that causes money to be created and put into circulation. And, of course, it is the act of paying off the debt that makes the money disappear. Like the trick of a magician, money appears out of nowhere and disappears without leaving the slightest trace.

Sir Josiah Stamp, governor of the Bank of England and who at the time was the second richest man in Britain in the 1920s, spoke about the modern banking system in a chat at the University of Texas in 1927:

"The modern banking system makes money out of nowhere. The process is perhaps the most surprising piece of prestidigitation ever invented. Banking was conceived in inequality and was born in sin. The bankers are really the owners of the land. Take it off, leaving them the power to create money and, with the smooth movement of a pen; create enough money to buy it again. Remove them this great power and all the great fortunes, including mine, would disappear, and then this would be a better and happier world to live. But, if they want to remain the slaves of the bankers and pay

the cost of their own slavery, then that the bankers continue to create the money and control the credit. "

As we will see in this chapter, the biggest deception of all is that there is no money in the system, only debts. Virtually all of the money supply currently consists of the debt we all have with private banks for the money they created out of nowhere using the accounting records in their books. All this is just a smoke screen and, to realize that it is simply a magic trick, we must look at it many times before discovering what is really happening. But when we manage to decipher this well hidden secret, everything around us changes and takes a new perspective.

THE FEDERAL RESERVE REVEALS THE SECRET OF THE MODERN BANKING

In a revealing brochure first published by the Federal Reserve of Chicago in 1961 and last updated in 1992, entitled *"Modern Money Mechanics: an exercise book on bank reserves and the expansion of deposits"*, It explains how money really works through the Federal Reserve System and, therefore, in practically all the central banks of the world. Here are some main ideas contained in the brochure:

"The real process of creating money takes place mainly in commercial banks. The banks do not really grant the loans of the money they receive as deposits. If you did this, you could not create additional money. What they do when they give loans, is to accept promissory notes in exchange for credits to the transaction accounts of the borrower [...] In the United States, neither paper money nor deposits have value as commodities. Intrinsically, a dollar bill is just

a piece of paper. The deposits are not really money either, they are only countable entries. The coins do have something of intrinsic value, mainly as metals, but their real value is much less than what people believe.

What makes these instruments -checks, paper money, deposits, and coins- accepted for trade and used in the economy, it is the confidence that people have that they can use them to exchange them for goods and services whenever they want. This works like this because a government law allows it. Money is currently called "money by decree"; therefore, it must be accepted ".

This brochure reveals the following: contrary to popular belief, *loans become deposits, and not vice versa*. That brings us back to one of the main ideas in this book.

MODERN MONEY IS DEBT

It is very difficult for people to understand that the total supply of money is only backed by debts, and it is even more amazing to visualize that, *if everyone paid their debts, all modern money would disappear*. There would be no money left in existence. The ATMs would stop working and the banks would close their doors. If we all pay the debts, we would enter a depression worse than that of 1929. If we all get into debt, the money supply expands. If we all pay the debts and stop borrowing, the money supply contracts and the depression begin.

Have you ever wondered: If we are all in debt and all the governments of the world also have strong debts, to whom are we all paying interest? The answer is: *all of us, including governments, are indebted to private banks.* Do you want to know what is the "cruel joke" of all this? The governments are indebted, and put to pay the debt to the taxpayers, for money created on a computer screen; money that they could have created themselves.

MONEY IS JUST AN ILLUSION

Wright Patman, who in the past was a Texas Congressman and chairman of the United States House Committee on Banking and Currency, decided one day to clarify his doubts about how money actually works. He went to a Federal Reserve bank, and when he was attended, I asked to see the money in cash. Bank officials who were on duty were quite confused and did not understand what to do. Patman repeated the request, only to be shown some of the bank's books and checks. Stunned and incredulous, he wrote the following:

"Cash money, in reality, does not exist and has never existed. What we call 'cash reserves' are simply credit in book entries in the books of the Federal Reserve Banks. These credits are created by the Federal Reserve Banks, and then they are passed through the banking system until they finally end up in the economy.

The Federal Reserve does not receive money, but creates it. When the Federal Reserve draws a check for a government bond, it does exactly what any bank does: it creates pure money simply by signing a check. When the beneficiary of the check wants cash, the Federal Reserve can accommodate it by printing cash, that is, Federal Reserve notes, which the beneficiary's commercial bank can deliver to him. The Federal Reserve, in short, is a complete money-making machine. "

THE TRUE ILLUSIONISTS: THE COMMERCIAL BANKS

The central bank of a country is indispensable for the printing of bankers' money. However, the money created today by central banks and governments is only a small portion of the total money supply. Most of the money that exists today is created by private commercial banks, through the Fractional Reserve System.

Let's start at the beginning. The "money supply" is defined as the total amount of notes, coins, loans, credits and other liquid instruments in the economy of a country. In other words, it's all the money in existence in the economy. The money supply of the United States is officially divided into M1, M2 and M3.

M1 is what first happens to people when they think about money: bills, coins and money in our checking accounts.

M2 is equal to M1 plus savings accounts, short-term investments of common money funds, and other types of deposits.

M3 is M1 and M2 plus institutional deposits, other long-term deposits and dollars circulating abroad.

For 2006, the last year in which the Fed shared with the M3 public, in the United States the Federal Reserve and the tangible currency represented only 2.4% of the total money supply, that is, M3. The other 97.6%, which appeared by magic, was created by commercial banks when they granted loans. Why did the Fed stop publishing M3 that year? Because at that time, the global financial crisis of 2008 was already beginning to bubble up and the Fed had to intervene by printing massive amounts of money. That is to say, if they had continued publishing the table and the graphs of M3, the money supply would have been overwhelmed by the policy they implemented at that time, called "Quantitative Easing". We will talk about this later.

THE IMPOSSIBLE CONTRACT

All of the above leads us to ask the following: If all the money that exists was born as a loan with a bank, where does the money come from to pay the interest to the bank? If the bank gives you a loan of $ 100,000 at 8%, you owe the bank $ 108,000. But the bank only created $ 100,000 for the loan. So, where are you going to get the interest? This dilemma is what is termed as *"the impossible contract"*.

Bernard Lietaer collaborated designing the euro, and has written several important books on monetary reform. He explains the impossible contract problem in the following way:

"When a bank gives you a mortgage loan of $ 100,000, you only create the capital, which you spend and then circulate in the economy. The bank expects you to pay $ 200,000 over the next 20 years, but do not create the other $ 100,000 (interest). Instead, the bank sends him to the cruel world to battle against everyone else to bring back the other $ 100,000. "

All this forces us to conclude the following: in the current monetary system, where money exists only for loans granted by banks with interest, *someone must obligatorily default on the payment of their debt so that another can pay it satisfactorily.*

To understand the problem of the impossible contract, let's analyze the ways in which we can "fulfill" this contract. Imagine that a bank lends us $ 10,000 to 9%, so we owe the bank $ 10,900. Since the bank only created $ 10,000, it seems that there is no way we can pay the debt with their respective interests. The amount of money put into circulation is not enough to cover the total debt, including interest. The only option we would have would be to borrow $ 900 to pay the interest. However, these $ 900 would have their own interests. Thus, *the more we borrow, the more we have to borrow just to address the interests, and the Fiat money-based debt is an endless spiral that leads to more and more debt. This is the reason why the public debt of practically all countries continues to expand non-stop: because it can never be paid. It is mathematically impossible. We are enslaved to continue borrowing money from banks, just to be able to pay interest.*

All of the above is a partial truth. While it is true that there is not enough money in circulation to cover the total interest, there is another way that we can get to pay without having to incur more debt: working.

THE MODERN SLAVERY

Let's assume that for the debt of $10,000 you have to pay monthly $ 900, of which $ 80 represent interest. Once the bill for the first month arrives, you understand that you are very pressured to make your payments, so you decide to look for a part-time job. On the other hand, the bank is earning $ 80 each month for your loan in the form of interest. Since these $ 80 are classified as "interests," the amount of the loan itself does not decrease. It is not a credit to capital. Therefore, this money is available for the bank to spend at will. In a meeting where they discuss what to do with the money, the decision is reached to have it implemented to wax the floors of the bank once a week. You find out about the new job opportunity there is, and the bank hires you for $ 80 a month. The result is that you earn the money to pay the interest on your loan, and the money you receive is exactly the same as you previously paid. As long as you stay doing the work required by the bank, the same dollars come into the bank as interest, and then they become your salary and then return to the bank as payment for the loan. At this point, you have stopped being a human to become a hamster that spins on a wheel without stopping. No matter how fast the hamster goes, the wheel always remains in the same place.

To better illustrate the previous example, we assumed that you worked directly for the bank, although this is not necessary. The disturbing fact that you must understand is that *it does not matter where you win the money, its origin was the bank and your final destination will be the bank.* The trip of that money can be long or short, but in the end, all the interest is paid eventually by human effort. And the discovery of that fact is surprising: *in the end, all human effort is for the sole and exclusive benefit of those who create the Fiat money, that is, the bankers.* This is the modern slavery that is happening now and that would not have been possible if the banks could not create Fiat money out of nowhere. The great mass of society gets up very early every day, drives for 40 minutes to get to the office, sits at his desk to work hard for more than ten hours, then drives back to his house and repeats this same pattern all week throughout the year, being a loyal servant of the ruling class composed of the financial elite.

HOW THE MAGICIANS CREATE THE ILLUSION OF MODERN MONEY

There are three ways in which the Federal Reserve can create Fiat money magically. The first is by making loans to members of private banks through something called the "Discount window". The second way is buying Treasury Bonds, Treasury Notes, Treasury Bills or any debt instrument issued by the government through what is known as the "Open Market Committee". The third way is by modifying the reserve ratio that the other bankers are obliged to maintain. Just as "all roads lead you to Rome," all the methods named above are simply different paths to reach the same goal: turn debt into money. Let's study the most used and complex roads, the first and the second, carefully.

THE DISCOUNT WINDOW

When banks begin to fall short of cash, the Central Bank intervenes by acting as a "lender of last resort" to inject all the necessary liquidity. Banks sometimes fall short of cash for several reasons: customers start demanding more cash, checks are going to other banks at the same time, or have made many bad loans that are going into default at the same time. Even so, the most obvious reason why banks borrow from the Central Bank is to make a profit. When the Central Bank lends money at a rate of 1%, banks lend this money at a much higher rate and thus make a profit. Although this is only the beginning. Consider the following example.

When a commercial bank borrows a dollar from the Federal Reserve, it becomes a "reserve" dollar. Assuming that banks are required to hold 10% reserves only, they can lend $ 9 for every dollar the Fed lends them. The math of this would work as follows:

Let's assume that the commercial bank receives $ 1 million from the Fed at an interest rate of 8%. The total annual cost for borrowing that money would be $ 80,000. The bank treats the loan as if it were a cash deposit, which means that it becomes the basis to create an additional $ 9 million dollars that can be lent to customers (see chapter 1 for the section that says *"how to creates debt through the fractional reserve banking system "*). If we assume that commercial banks lend that money to 11%, their *gross return* would be $ 990,000. After covering the $ 80,000 interest that must be paid to the Federal Reserve plus some additional expenses, the *net return* would be $ 900,000. I'll put it in the following way: The bank borrows $ 1 million dollars and can almost double it in a year. Speaking of leverage! And remember the source of that leverage: the bank's ability to create $ 9 million dollars out of nowhere that passes through the banking system and then add to the country's economy.

OPEN MARKET COMMITTEE

This is the method most used by the Federal Reserve and central banks to create Fiat money. They do it by buying government debt with money newly created for that purpose. The consequences of implementing this mechanism are surprising. To the "Open Market Committee", I like to call it *"The House of Paper"*. You will already realize why.

MONEY HEIST

For this section, I must give credit to G. Edward Griffin, who explains this topic like nobody else and clarifies this obscure and confusing scheme so that anyone can understand it. Before continuing, let me give you a few words of warning: do not expect the explanation I am about to give you to make any sense. In fact, the more intelligent and honest you are, the harder it will be to understand what comes next. Just accept and try to understand that this is how the printing press of bank magicians works. The trick they use is to use words and phrases that have meanings very different from those that the average person knows. Be very careful with words. They are not there to explain what really happens, but to deceive and repel the mind of any intruder who tries to discover the best kept secret of banking. Once you study it carefully and avoid falling into the traps where most people fall, you will understand the following: the process by which a central bank - in this case the Federal Reserve - creates money is not at all complicated. It is simply absurd. No more to add, I present you *"MONEY HEIST"*:

Name of the game: Money Heist.

Objective of the game: Turn debt into money.

Participants: Central bankers, commercial banks, politicians, taxpayers and citizens.

Team 1: Central bankers, commercial banks and politicians.

Team 2: Taxpayers and citizens.

Description: Money Heist is an unequal game. One team knows the rules of the game, while the other does not. Team 2 is a simple victim of the game. Team 1 must create a magic mechanism through which they can create massive amounts of money without Team 2 get to know. Team 1 can use everything in its power to confuse Team 2 and achieve its goal. Confusing words, rare mechanisms, acts of prestidigitation, and any nonsense that comes to mind is valid to confuse and deceive the public. Team 2 must do everything possible to discover the trick of these magicians who use their political puppets to remain hidden behind the scenes orchestrating the entire show. If Team 2 discover the trick and wake up from the illusion, everything will be seen as what it really is: a fraud. If this happens, Team 2 wins the game and bankers and politicians cannot continue taking money out of an empty hat. If Team 1 wins the game, Team 2 will be plunged into debt slavery, taxes and inflation.

Instructions: The objective is to turn government debt into money. As simple as that. First, the central bank, which in this case will be the Federal Reserve, takes all the Government Bonds, Notes and Letters (promissory notes) that the public does not buy and writes a check to Congress in exchange for them. There is no money to support this check that Congress received from the Fed. These Fiat dollars are created on the act for this particular purpose. The Fed calls these bonds "reserves," and uses them as the basis to create nine additional dollars (assuming that is the fractional reserve) for every dollar created by the same bonds. The money that Congress received in exchange for bonds and other debt instruments is spent by the government, while the money created on top of those bonds is the source of all bank loans made for people and businesses in the country. All this could be simplified by simply turning on a printing press and starting to create money, but that would be cheating in the game and Team 1 would be disqualified. Team 1 must remember the challenge that makes this game meaningful: it must cheat Team 2 and make the illusion of creating money is based on an accounting trick instead of a printed trick.

Now, let's start playing. Everything starts with...

DEBT OF THE GOVERNMENT

The federal government takes a piece of paper, adds ink, creates some amazing designs around the edges and at the end of the process calls this paper a "Treasure Bonus" or a "Treasury Note", or a "Treasury Bill" " All these papers are simple promises to pay a specific amount of money at a specific interest, during a specific period of time. It is what is known as "pagare" or IOU (in English I

Owe You, or Te Debo). In the past, as we saw in the first chapter, the basis on which all the money was created was the gold or silver that the bankers kept in different vaults. However, at present, the so-called "reserves" are these debt instruments. These pieces of paper that the government issues in exchange for the Fed's money eventually become the basis for almost all of the nation's money supply. What the government has done by issuing these promissory notes, really, is to create cash. The trick is that it still does not look like money, much less cash. Turning this debt into paper bills and checkbook money is the function of the central bank, that is, of the Federal Reserve. For this transformation from debt to money to be successful, that Bond, Note or Letter from the government is delivered to the Fed, where it is then classified as...

ASSETS

A government debt instrument is considered an asset throughout the world because it is assumed that the government will keep its promise to pay. This assumption is based on the fact that the government is able to obtain all the money it needs through taxes. Therefore, what makes this piece of paper, whether it be a Bond, a Note or a Letter from the government, a solid asset, is the lender's assurance that he will be paid. Now that we clarify the reason why a paper with good designs is an asset, the Federal Reserve uses it to balance its books, that is, it now has an "asset" that can be used to offset a liability. Next, create this liability by adding ink to another piece of paper and exchange it with the government for the asset. That second piece of paper is a...

CHECK OF THE FEDERAL RESERVE

If you or I issued a check without funds, we would go to prison for fraud. However, for the Federal Reserve and the other central banks it is completely legal. The check they issue to buy the government debt does not have any funds; it does not exist any bank deposit against which the document can be changed. When the Federal Reserve issues a check, it is making money. The funds of the check are created at the time the check was issued. The reason why Fed can do this is because Congress wants the money, and knows that raising taxes directly to get it would be the equivalent of political suicide. It also knows that no one else is able to buy all the bonds he issues, especially when the interest rates paid by these bonds are very low. And finally, if Congress decides to print massive amounts of money instead of disguising everything through the banking system, it would be very obvious the nature of Fiat money and it would cause much controversy.

Operating in this way, therefore, the process is hidden under an aura of mystery in the banking system. Obviously, the final result would be the same if the government simply decided to turn on the printing press and start making Fiat money to cover all their expenses.

To continue with the illusion, now it is said that the books are "balanced", because the "liability", which is the money that the Fed issued, is compensated by the "asset", which in this case is the promissory note that Congress gave to the Fed in exchange for the check. The Federal Reserve check is now endorsed and the government sends it back again to one of the Federal Reserve banks, where it now becomes...

DEPOSIT OF THE GOVERNMENT

After the Federal Reserve's check has been deposited in the Government's account, this is used to pay the government's expenses and, therefore, it transforms into many...

GOVERNMENT CHECKS

These checks become the means by which the first round of Fiat money floods the economy. Addresses now deposit them in their own bank accounts where they become...

DEPOSITS IN THE COMMERCIAL BANKS

Bank deposits immediately take on a divided personality. Looking at them on the one hand, they are liabilities for the bank because they should be returned to the depositors when they need them. But, while they remain in the bank, they are also considered as assets because they are at hand. In this way the books are balanced again because the assets compensate the liabilities. Next, the show begins. Through the magic of the fractional reserve, the deposits are destined to fulfill a purpose much more lucrative. Deposits are now reclassified in books and take the name of...

BANK RESERVES

Why do they take the name of reserves? Is it to pay the depositors in case they want to close their accounts and get their money back? No. That function was fulfilled before. Now that they are considered "reserves", they become the basis through which massive amounts of Fiat money are built. Here begins the real action: at the level of commercial banks. This is how the trick works. The banks have the permission of the Fed to keep only 10% of their deposits in "reserve" (this usually varies). That means that, if they receive deposits of $ 1 million dollars from the first round of Fiat money created by the Fed, they have $ 900,000 more than what they are required to keep on hand. If we use the bankers' vocabulary, those $ 900,000 are called...

EXCESS RESERVES

The word "excess" is interesting. It means that these so-called reservations are destined to fulfill a special mission. Now that they are considered an excess, they are considered available for loans. Therefore, when the indicated moment arrives, these excess reserves become...

BANK LOANS

Let's stop for a minute to contemplate something. If this money is owned by the original depositors, who can write checks and spend it any time they want, how can it be borrowed? Would not this cause a double claim against the same money? No, because the trick is that, when the new loans are made, they are not made with the deposits that the banks have in hand. They are made with money newly manufactured out of nowhere for this purpose. The money supply of a country increases 90% of the deposits of the banks, assuming a fractional reserve of 10% as in this case. Additionally, the new money that appeared by magic art is much more interesting for bankers than the old money. The old money, which they received from depositors, requires them to pay interest or perform additional services for having the privilege of using it. But, with the new money, for which they did not have to work and save to own it, banks charge interest and make substantial profits. Not bad, considering that it just appeared by magic. The process is still far from over. When this second round of Fiat money (the newly created bank loans) comes into circulation in the economy, it returns to the banking system again, just as the first round did, in the form of...

MORE DEPOSITS IN THE COMMERCIAL BANKS

This process can be better visualized in chapter 1 with the fractional reservation process table that we analyze. It works exactly the same, except that in this example the fractional reserve is 10%, while in the example of chapter 1 the fractional reserve was 20%. Although the numbers change, the process and the concept remain the same. If you're having trouble understanding it, get together with a friend and study this process with the table in Chapter 1 at hand.

Going back to the point, the money machine continues working, but now with slightly smaller numbers in each round. What was a "loan" on Friday, returns to the bank as a "deposit" on Monday. The deposit is then reclassified as a "reserve" and 90% of that becomes an "excess" reserve that, once again, is available for a new "loan". So, the million dollars of the first round of Fiat money gives birth to $ 900,000 in the second round, and those $ 900,000 give birth to $ 810,000 in the third round. This process is repeated many times more, where deposits become loans and then become deposits that once again become loans until, finally, the process reaches the maximum level, which is ...

BANK FIAT MONEY: 9 TIMES THE DEBT OF THE GOVERNMENT

The amount of Fiat money created by commercial banks throughout this process, working with a fractional reserve of 10%, is approximately nine times the amount of the original government debt that made the whole process possible in the first place. After adding the original debt to this figure, we finally have...

TOTAL FIAT MONEY: 10 TIMES THE DEBT OF THE GOVERNMENT

The total amount of Fiat money that can be created by the Federal Reserve and the other commercial banks together is approximately ten times the amount of the underlying public debt. As you see, the basis of the world economy is neither gold nor silver, but the debt we all have with banks. That's why the subtitle is *how to use debt and taxes to get rich,* because, as I just showed you, modern money is nothing but debt. All the money that the banks create floods the economy, which inevitably far exceeds the goods and services. *When the money supply (that is, the amount of money in existence) exceeds the goods and services of the economy, inflation is inevitable.* The effect of this is that the purchasing power of all money, old and new, decreases as banks artificially make money. At this point, it is easy to realize the following: *practically nothing rises in value or "appreciates", what really happens is that the prices of assets, products and services go up because the value of money has gone down.* In reality, it is a kind of "deflation" of the currency that appears in our lives with a facade of "inflation", where the devaluation of money causes the supposed appreciation of everything else. It would have been the same as stealing this purchasing power from taxes directly. But, doing it through inflation, which is a hidden tax, the whole process becomes imperceptible to the masses. So, the reality is that all this is a...

HIDDEN TAX

Without realizing it, we have paid throughout all the years in which the central banks are in operation, in addition to the normal taxes, a completely hidden tax equivalent to many times the national debt. And we still do not reach the end of the process. Since the source of all our money is a lot of debt, its amount can increase or decrease. When we all become more indebted and interest rates go down, the nation's money supply expands, prices rise and we feel prosperous. But when the debts are paid off, the interest rates go up and nobody else wants to get into debt, the money supply contracts, the prices go down and the recession begins. In a nutshell: *The Federal Reserve System can lead us to hyperinflation or a depression due to deflation depending on how it acts.* If you buy many government debt instruments, lower interest rates and encourage cheap debt, release the reins so that you start an inflationary bubble that you will eventually have to stop in the future and, when you do, it will be implementing the opposite that you did in first place, it will sell the government debt instruments it has, it will raise interest rates and restrict credit. This would inevitably lead us to a deflation that could turn into a depression. This alternation between periods of expansion and contraction of the money supply is the underlying cause of...

AUGES, CRACKS AND DEPRESSIONS

Obviously, this greatly affects the average citizen, since he falls into the trap of cheap credit and the "wealth effect", which occurs when assets are increasing a lot of value, and then, without warning, being pushed into the monetary contraction and the devaluation of assets when the central bank decides that it is time to stop the inflationary bubble and cut off credit.

The real beneficiaries are the politicians, who enjoy having an unlimited income account whenever they want to perpetuate their power, and bankers kings within the largest cartel that exists called the Central Bank, which charge interest in perpetuity for nothing.

Of course, politicians and bankers will never tell you this. They are very skilled people who know how to handle this type of situation and have become very skilled in the art of deceiving the public. They have a whole speech planned for when the game they are playing with us gets out of hand: *"This kind of thing happens naturally. Booms and collapses in the economy are natural cycles, such as summer and winter. There is no master plan. Do not listen to those lunatics who think this is a conspiracy. Simply, there is no one to blame. It's all under control. Sooner than you imagine, things will return to normal. Relax, go back to work, pay your taxes on time, keep borrowing money, and go back to sleep immediately, slave!"*

End of the game? For now, yes.

The game we just described was played assuming a reserve of 10%. However, we must keep in mind that this is purely arbitrary. Since the money is Fiat and we already know well the characteristics of this type of money, we do not have a backing in gold or silver that limits its impression, the only reason that exists is what it considers convenient for the bankers in charge. If you are in your place, more money will be allocated to the affiliated banks or your political friends, the reserve may fall completely. Thus, *there is no limit to the amount of Fiat money that can be manufactured under the current banking system.*

INDEBTED FOR LIFE AND HOSTAGES OF THIS SYSTEM

The politicians in Congress who issue the debt in exchange for the Federal Reserve checks, and the bankers who collaborate in this whole process, know what is really happening and that you have probably overlooked while reading these pages. What we have called "government debt" or "national debt", that is, the Bonds, Notes or Treasury Bills that the Fed buys, are not really debt instruments. It is not a true debt, for the simple fact that no one in Washington or whatever the capital of the country involved really expects to ever pay it. Governments cannot pay the debt they have with central banks and extract their values because then there would be no bonds to back all the money issued by the bank. In a few words, if a government proposes to pay its national debt and gets it, all the money in the economy would disappear. Let's review why this is so.

Every dollar, euro, yen, peso, Yuan or pound that exists at this time, was created by the simple act of the loan. Someone had to borrow the money we used to come into existence, be it the government, commercial banks, foreign governments, corporations, or simply us when we applied for a mortgage to buy our home or a credit for our car. Therefore, if all the debts were paid and no one else will go into debt, all our money supply would disappear again in the computers. The national debt, that is, the debt that the government gave to the central bank in exchange for the checks, is the main basis on which money is created for the private debt. If the government pays its debt or even reduces it considerably, that it would be enough for our monetary system to be paralyzed. Even if there were sufficient funds to pay the debt, no politician would dare to support this, since it would be the end of the economy as we know it today. Remember the following:

- The purchase of Bonds, Notes, or Treasury Bills (i.e., government debt instruments) by the Federal Reserve or a central bank (with a check with nothing to back it up), creates money.
- The sale of Bonds, Notes, or Treasury Bills, extinguishes the money.

The most serious consequence of having implemented the modern banking system and granting the power to the banks to create the money of a nation, is that from the moment it was implemented and got into operation, the government and all of us were entangled in a cobweb of debt. It is impossible for us to pay off the debt we have with the bankers. Please, re-read the above. It is not an exaggeration. It is something that has already been demonstrated mathematically.

Therefore, public debt not only cannot be paid, but must be continually expanded. The banking system forces governments to borrow more and more and exceed projected budgets. This is what Marriner Eccles, Governor of the Federal Reserve Board, confessed in the hearings before the Committee of the Chamber for the Bank and the Currency in 1941.

Wright Patman asked Eccles how the Federal Reserve got the money to buy the government bonds. The conversation went something like this:

Eccles: We created it.

Patman: From what?

Eccles: Of the right that we have to issue money-debt.

Patman: And there is nothing behind that money, except the credit of our government?

Eccles: This is how our banking system and economy work. *If there were no debts, there would be no money.*

This is the reason why the public debt does not stop increasing and, in the United States, the federal debt has not been paid for almost two centuries. Practically every year the government has exceeded its projected budget, thus increasing the national debt. The economist John Kenneth Galbraith wrote referring to this situation, in 1975, the following:

*"Several years after the Civil War, the Federal Government recorded a large surplus. But he faced a dilemma: he could not pay his debt or withdraw the titles, because doing so meant there would be no bonds to back national bank notes. **Paying the debt meant destroying the money supply. "***

The federal debt has been the basis of the entire money supply of the United States since the Civil War, when a law was passed that allowed private banks to issue their own banknotes backed by government bonds that were deposited in the Treasury of the United States. Therefore, since then, the money in existence could not exist without the federal debt. Both were needed to live. If the debt disappeared, the money too. In order to keep all the money within the economic system, some heavy player has to incur a substantial debt that can never be paid, and this role is gladly assumed by the government. For this reason the federal debt has not been paid in almost two centuries and on the contrary it does not stop increasing.

DEFICITS BECOME SOMETHING "NORMAL"

In the 1980s, the authorities openly declared that "deficits do not matter". That means that the government can incur the "deficit spending" and simply allow the debt to grow as needed without any fuss. This policy continues today. Given that the debt is impossible to pay and that trying to do this or even reduce it could mean the end of the economy as we know it, it is not surprising that the people in charge now consider that spending more than they earn is a normal practice. The danger of this is that if the debt overflows and the government cannot even face the interests, there will come a day where they will communicate the following: "We are very sorry. This time we fell short. We will not be able to meet our payments and we will have to renege the debt. "The day the United States insinuates at least that it is not in the capacity to pay interest on its debt, the economy of the whole world would collapse. In a later chapter we will discuss the danger in which the United States is currently having embarked on the train of deficit spending.

What does deficit spending have to do with the huge government debt and inflation with you and our world? How does this affect us day to day? In two main ways: the tax on income and inflation. Let's analyze both.

CLARIFYING THE LIE OF INCOME TAX

Before 1914 - the year the Federal Reserve came into operation - people paid very little tax and could keep 100% of their personal income, which meant they did not have to pay the well-known income tax. Despite all this, there were roads, hospitals, fire departments, police, armies and public schools. Why did this happen? Is not all this supposed to be paid with the taxpayers' money? That's what they want you to believe so that you pay your taxes on time.

On December 22, 1913, Congress renounced its constitutional right to issue money and regulate its value, and handed it over to the Federal Reserve - a private corporation - when it approved the Federal Reserve Act. When this new law entered Operating in 1914, each of the dollars that the Fed manufactured was to be paid again with their respective interests. *Since the government did not generate enough revenue to cover the interest that was due to the Federal Reserve, the income tax was created.* In summary:

- From 1914, every dollar exists only because someone borrowed it.
- We pay interest for every dollar that exists.
- That interest is paid to the Federal Reserve, which is a private bank and pays dividends to its shareholders.
- The most powerful banking consortiums in the world are the owners of the Federal Reserve, so the interest we pay through taxes ends up in the pockets of the richest and most influential families in the world.

- It is impossible to pay the debt for two reasons: it is mathematically impossible, and even if it were possible, paying the debt would make all the modern money disappear. The only thing we can do is to continue asking for more loans to pay interest and to get entangled more and more in the web of debt.
- The government created the income tax to pay the interest.

Welcome, for the first time, to the real world.

The US government took 198 years to borrow the first billion dollars. Then, in just twelve years, he borrowed another 3 billion. In 2018, the public debt of the United States reached a historical record, exceeding $ 21 billion. This data is provided by the United States Department of the Treasury. To better understand the magnitude of this debt, in 2011, the United States paid more than $ 14,000 per second only in interest on the debt. The same year, in total, he paid more than $ 454 billion dollars in interest on his federal debt. Currently, interest payments represent the largest government expenditure, surpassing even that of Defense and the combined cost of the departments of Agriculture, Education, Energy, Housing and Urban Development, Transportation and Veterans Affairs.

All that mountain of money that is destined to pay the interest of the debt that the government issued comes out of the pocket of the taxpayers, in the form of taxes and inflation. That money you are confiscated is not used to provide government services, or to pay previous debts. Nothing is produced with that money, not even roads or government buildings. It is not used for welfare or medical benefits. No wages are paid with this money. It does not serve to uphold the standard of living of the nation. It is not used to improve education or invest in the development of the country. The harsh reality is that this money does absolutely nothing except pay interest.

In addition, interest on the debt is compound, which means that, even if the government completely stopped its deficit spending, the total debt would continue to rise as a result of the interests of that part that already exists. In 2006, interest on the national debt already consumed almost 40% of all income collected from personal income taxes.

Do not you think it's incredible? Without interest on the national debt, taxes on personal income and corporate taxes could decrease considerably or, even, disappear completely. The most incredible thing is that with $ 267 billion dollars we would end world hunger, according to a study carried out by the United Nations Food and Agriculture Organization, the International Fund for Agricultural Development and the World Food Program. After making a rigorous study, they came to the following conclusion:

"Our study estimates that eradicating hunger will require a total investment of about $ 267 billion dollars per year over the next 15 years. Given that this is roughly equivalent to 0.3% of world GDP, we believe it is a relatively small price to pay to end chronic hunger. "

Tarek El Diwany is a British expert in finance, who revealed several years ago what was happening in the world at a presentation in Cambridge:

Unfortunately, under the current system and the policies that are implemented in the financial system, it is a utopia to think that taxes will decrease and that the money that is created from out of nowhere will stop going into the pockets of bankers and begin to go to causes that truly make this world a better place. People must continue living within their income and not exceed, in order to pay taxes to a government that is unable to live within their income and all they know is innovative ways to exceed. Politicians cover many expenses, not with taxes, but with the sale of government bonds, further deepening the debt each year and condemning the future of future generations.

Richard Russell, financial analyst, pointed out in his April 2005 bulletin the following:

"When the government of the United States needs money, it collects it through taxes or the issuance of bonds. These bonds are sold to the Fed and this in turn makes deposits in the form of accounting entries. This "money-debt" created out of nowhere is then available to the government. But if the government can issue Treasury Bills, Notes and Bonds, it can also issue currency, as it did before it was approved by the Federal Reserve. If the United States issued its own money, it could cover all its expenses, and income tax would not be necessary. So, what is the objection to getting rid of the Fed and letting the US government issue its own currency? Simple, it leaves the bankers out and eliminates the income tax. "

It is important to understand this, since many people consider that paying tax is "a patriotic act" or is "the price we must pay to live in a civilized society." It's false. Taxes, for the most part, end up in the hands of bankers and politicians. Starting from this idea, in the second part of this book I will show you how to reduce or even eliminate the taxes you pay for your income and your investments, all in a legal way. The key is to learn to play with the same bankers' rules: turn debt into money and collect interest for money created from out of nowhere. Even if you do not believe me, you can do the same. You can build your own printing press. All you have to do is learn to use the debt and taxes in your favor. Later we will analyze how.

CHEATING IN MONOPOLY

Some friends meet and sit down to play Monopoly. Naturally, one of them will be the banker. They want the game to be real, so they give the banker a special power: he can print all the money he wants and he has no limit to the amount of money he can distribute. Every time he throws the dice, draws another stack of paper money under the table that all players must use as money. As the banker is also one of the players (as in our real world), obviously, as the game progresses, the other players will realize the terrible mistake they made: no matter what happens or in which box it falls, since the moment he obtained the power to manage the money supply of the game, he emerged victorious. The banker, inevitably, will end up being the owner of all properties. But, while that happens, the increasing flood of money caused by the banker affects all the players. As the amount of money becomes larger, the relative value of each bill decreases, and property prices rise as a result of this.

The game is called "Monopoly" for a reason. In the end, one person will have all the properties and the others will be bankrupt. But it does not matter. After all, it's just a game, right?

Unfortunately, it is not a game in the real world. We are talking about our home, our food and the welfare of society. Winning Monopoly simply because you have the power to create money at will makes all the difference. Every time a new dollar is printed and spent, the bank keeps all the purchasing power of that dollar. But where does the purchasing power come from? It was stolen from your dollars in secret. Every time a new bill comes into circulation, it devalues all other existing bills, because now there is more money to acquire the same amount of goods and services. It's the law of supply and demand. This causes prices to increase and become the deceitful hidden tax that we know as inflation. Whenever something seems to be on the rise, be it stocks, real estate, commodities or any type of asset that you can think of, you cannot lose your head and you should ask yourself: "Why is it going up in value? Any significant change or improvement to explain this sudden increase? Or has everything remained more or less the same and it seems to be valuing itself by magic? "The reason why everything seems to go up continuously is because central and commercial banks" inject liquidity "into the economy, increasing the money supply and provoking everything goes up ... except the money itself! In general, if everything is becoming more expensive, it is because the currency in question is going down. The inherent value of a product, a service or an asset usually never changes, what happens is that having more currency in circulation, its value is diluted, so more foreign currency is required to acquire them.

We have come a long way unmasking the monster that was born in London, took his first steps on Jekyll Island, and reached adulthood recently. There is still much to know about his existence and we will have to continue traveling in time to know his most precious moments and the way they affect our lives. It is important to know his history and the achievements he has achieved; only then, we can defeat him at his own game.

SUMMARY

- Money does not exist, there are only debts. It is not until someone borrows money and spends it when it comes into circulation in the economy. It is the act of borrowing that causes money to be created and put into circulation. And, of course, it is the act of paying off the debt that makes the money disappears. Like the trick of a magician, money appears out of nowhere and disappears without leaving the slightest trace.

- Contrary to popular belief, loans become deposits, not the other way around.

- If everyone paid their debts, modern money would disappear.

- All of us, including governments, are indebted to private banks. Do you want to know what is the "cruel joke" of all this? The governments are indebted, and put to pay the debt to the taxpayers, for money created on a computer screen; money that they could have created themselves.

- Cash money, in reality, does not exist and has never existed. What we call the "cash reserves" are simply credits in book entries in the books of the Federal Reserve Banks. These credits are created by the Federal Reserve Banks and then passed through the banking system until eventually ending up in the economy.

- The money created today by central banks and governments is only a small portion of the total money supply. Most of the money that exists today is created by private commercial banks, through the Fractional Reserve System.

- In the current monetary system, where money exists only for the loans granted by banks with interest, someone must obligatorily default on the payment of their debt so that another can pay it satisfactorily.

- The more we borrow, the more we have to borrow just to face the interests, and the Fiat money-based debt is an endless spiral that leads to more and more debt. This is the reason why the public debt of practically all countries continues to expand non-stop: because it can never be paid. It is mathematically impossible. We are enslaved to continue borrowing money from banks, just to be able to pay interest.

- It does not matter where you earn your money, its origin was the bank and its final destination will be the bank. The trip of that money can be long or short, but in the end, all the interest is paid eventually by human effort. In the end, all human effort is for the sole and exclusive benefit of those who create the Fiat money, that is, the bankers.

- There are three ways in which the Federal Reserve can create Fiat money magically. The first is by making loans to members of private banks through something called the **"Discount window"**. The second way is buying government debt instruments through what is known as the **"Open Market Committee"**. The third way is by modifying the reserve ratio that the other bankers are obliged to maintain.

- Virtually nothing goes up in value or is "appreciated", what really happens is that the prices of assets, products and services go up because the value of money has gone down.

- There is no limit to the amount of Fiat money that can be manufactured under the current banking system.

- Every dollar, euro, yen, peso, Yuan or pound that exists at this time, was created by the simple act of the loan. Someone had to borrow the money we used to come into existence.

- If a government intends to pay its national debt and gets it, all the money in the economy would disappear.
- The national debt, that is, the debt that the government gave to the central bank in exchange for the checks, is the main basis on which money is created for the private debt. If the government pays its debt or even reduces it considerably, that would be enough for our monetary system to be paralyzed.
- If the public debt is overflowing and the government cannot even meet the interest, there will come a day where it will not be able to meet the payments and it will have to renege the debt. The day the United States insinuates at least that it is not able to pay interest on its debt; the economy of the whole world will collapse.
- Since the government did not generate enough revenue to cover the interest that was due to the Federal Reserve, the income tax was created.
- Welcome, for the first time, to the real world.

Chapter 4

The global financial crisis

"There is no more subtle and sure way to tear down the foundations of society, than to corrupt the currency. The process involves all the forces of economic law with destruction, and it does so in such a way that no man would be able to detect it. "

–*John Maynard Keynes*

The global financial crisis we have today is not an isolated event that happened overnight. It has been growing throughout the twentieth century. In this chapter we will discuss the most important events of that century and how bankers have come out as the great winners at the expense of others.

THE GREAT DEPRESSION

The stock market collapsed precipitously in 1929, causing a deep depression that lasted more than a decade. The collapse of 1929 was the largest bank stampede in history. Although the Fed had the task of preventing banking panics when it was approved back in 1913, it could not do anything and failed in its mission to protect the economy of the United States.

It all started in "the crazy twenties" and the euphoria of that time. The Federal Reserve reduced interest rates for a long time, making credit abundant and people get into debt much more easily.

People started buying cars, houses and all kinds of products on credit. The money was so simple to get that people who had no financial education and had never invested before were now borrowing large sums of cash just to invest. The public was sold the idea that they could use the stock market to get rich quickly. All they had to do was borrow money, buy shares and then sell them more expensive. On the stock exchange, buying shares with credit is called a *margin*. When buying margin, the investor is allowed to make an initial payment for their shares and pay the balance later when its price rises, thus obtaining profits. Of course, this speculative investment returned to the stock market a pyramid scheme, in which most of the money invested did not really exist. People opened margin accounts to leverage their investments and obtain better returns. This system drove the vast majority of people crazy, who could not see what was really happening. People began betting on their homes, their lifelong savings, life insurance and whatever they had within reach to not miss the "opportunity of their lives". The commercial banks took advantage of all this and offered mortgage loans with interest rates favorable to those naive who fell into the trap. The Federal Reserve made all this possible by substantially reducing the rediscount rate, that is, the interest rate paid by banks when borrowing from the Federal Reserve. The Federal Reserve made it easy for banks to acquire additional reserves, in order to be able to increase the number of loans several times thanks to the fractional reserve system.

Why did the Federal Reserve flood the economy with debt and refuse to intervene when the collapse came? After the First World War, the pound sterling had lost value against gold.

The result of this was a significant contraction of the British gold reserves. The Federal Reserve, to prevent gold from escaping from England to the United States, supported the Bank of England by keeping interest rates low and thus inflating the US dollar. Because London had higher interest rates, investors saw it as a more attractive place to park their gold, thus withdrawing it from the United States and taking it to England. The problem was that the low interest rates caused an inflation bubble that could not be controlled.

Representatives of the Bank of England and the Federal Reserve met frequently before the market sank in 1929. Evidence suggests that, in February 1929, both banks concluded that a collapse would be inevitable and that it would be best to let this it was corrected in a "natural" way, that is, without the help of the Fed or any type of intervention. Next, the Fed began selling bonds and other debt instruments in the open market, contracting the money supply. Remember that when the Fed buys bonds and government debt, its reserves increase and can support more loans. In a few words: when the Fed purchases debt, the money supply expands, and when the Fed sells debt, the money supply contracts. For a long time the Fed expanded the money supply by buying debt and lowering the rediscount rate. This caused an inflationary bubble. Now, to deflate the bubble, he did just the opposite: he began to reduce his reserves by selling public securities and he raised interest rates. These new Fed policies resulted in a liquidity crisis and a lack of available money. Since all the money in existence is born from the act of borrowing, by raising interest rates and reducing reserves, loans become more expensive and money in circulation is scarce. The loans were now available but at a much higher interest rate, causing people to stop buying shares at margin. As people stopped buying shares, their prices began to fall, putting investors who had acquired shares on margin (that is, with borrowed money) in a very dangerous situation. This caused that many investors had to sell at a lower price than they had bought, suffering heavy losses. The panic had begun, and the same rookies who rushed to buy to get rich quickly, were now rushed to sell before they lost everything. The bag collapsed practically from one day to the next. People withdrew their savings from banks in a massive way. Foreign investors took their gold elsewhere, further depleting the reserves on which the money supply had been built. The amount of money in circulation was reduced by one third from 1929 to 1933, and more than a half of the banks closed their doors during that same period. The Federal Reserve refused to intervene injecting liquidity into the economy and allowed people to go bankrupt and businesses to go bankrupt.

Only a small and select group, composed of those who had met on Jekyll Island in 1910, became incredibly rich during the Great Depression. Before the stock market collapsed and the Fed implemented the new monetary policies, the head of the Bank of England (Montagu Norman) and the governor of the New York Federal Reserve (Benjamin Strong) sent warning messages to the lists of their preferential clients, including wealthy industrialists, politicians and powerful bankers, telling them to leave the market immediately. These people left the market on time, selling their securities at the highest point and earning large profits. Then, when people panicked and began to sell, these same magnates bought the securities at the auction price again. While the novice investors jumped from the windows, the rich accumulated large packages of shares and real estate. *Wealth was not being destroyed, it was simply being transferred.* We must remember that the collapse of the prices of shares and real estate did not necessarily mean that these assets had something bad. Stocks still represented solid companies that continued to pay dividends and real estate still had strong demand and generated income. The intrinsic value of the assets had not changed, it was its price that had been altered. The price of the shares was inflated for a long time because the novices began to buy in heaps. When they started selling all at the same time, their price plummeted, but their value remained the same, because the companies that were behind the shares had not really changed. *The intrinsic value of the assets had not changed; it was their price that had been altered.* The price of the shares was inflated for a long time because the novices began to buy in heaps. When they started selling all at the same time, their price plummeted, but their value remained the same, because the companies that were behind the shares had not really changed.

The Great Depression was not accidental. The big Rockefeller and Morgan banks had now scrapped the competition, eliminating thousands of small banks that were forced to close their doors, just as had been planned on Jekyll Island. The panic caused by the bankers led the public to rely more and more on their services, and forced the government to take stronger measures to protect and favor the interests of the largest banks and the Federal Reserve. Louis T. McFadden, chairman of the Banking and Currency Committee of the House of Representatives, stated the following:

"Depression was not accidental. It was a carefully engineered event. The international bankers sought to generate here a state of despair in order to emerge as the sovereigns of all of us. "

Something you must understand about the depression of 1929 is that it was a depression by deflation, which means the following: since all the money in circulation was born through the act of borrowing, when the loans failed and the delinquency increased, the money disappeared. As people were unable to pay their loans, the money supply contracted, thousands of small banks closed, businesses went bankrupt and people lost their homes and savings. The crisis of 2008 began in the same way: the money supply contracted significantly because the indebtedness had been excessive and a very large portion of that debt could not be repaid. The difference is that, in 1929, the Federal Reserve did not print money to keep the economy afloat, and in 2008 it did. In the following pages we will talk about the most important events worldwide that led us to the crisis we have today.

BRETTON WOODS AND THE NEW ECONOMIC ORDER

The Bretton Woods Agreement was concluded in 1944, at the end of the Second World War, and gave birth to the International Monetary Fund, the World Bank and the new world reserve currency, the US dollar. The system that was implemented before this agreement had totally failed, since Great Britain and the United States, the world bankers, had run out of gold. Before Bretton Woods, the currencies were exchanged in terms of their value in gold, and the agreement was called "the gold exchange standard". This should not be confused with the "gold standard," which is where a currency is backed by gold. The gold exchange standard only meant that the exchange of the different currencies (most of which were not backed by gold) was determined by the amount of gold that they could buy in the market. What the new plan was looking for was to support gold with US dollars, which at that time were considered "as good as gold", and the United States would agree to keep its convertibility in gold at a fixed price of $ 35 dollars per ounce. As long as faith in the dollar was intact and everyone would stick to the agreement, there was little fear that gold would be scarce, because gold would not really be used.

The Bretton Woods Agreement stands out for the following:

- The International Monetary Fund was born to establish exchange rates.
- The World Bank was born to provide credit to countries devastated by war and developing countries in the Third World.
- The dollar was designated as a world reserve currency.
- The US dollar could be converted into gold at a price of $ 35 per ounce.
- Countries could convert their dollars into gold.

The New Economic Order had been established. However, the bankers would continue to shape it at will during the following years. Let's see how the facts developed.

THE BANKERS' DREAM COMES TRUE

For most of the twentieth century, bankers had two major obstacles that limited the amount of debt they could create in the United States. The first obstacle was the Federal Reserve's legal obligation to have gold to back a percentage of the paper money it issued. The second obstacle was the legal obligation of private commercial banks to have liquidity reserves to support their deposits. Both obstacles were eliminated satisfactorily, allowing the debt to grow exponentially and take hostage the economy as a whole. Let's start with the first one.

The Federal Reserve Act, which was approved in 1913, created the Federal Reserve System, the central bank of the United States, and was granted the power to issue Federal Reserve notes. However, that law had a requirement: the Fed should have "gold reserves not less than 40% in relation to their Federal Reserve notes in circulation in the economy". In other words, the Fed was required to have 40 cents in gold for every dollar bill it created. This relationship was subsequently reduced by Congress in 1945, dropping it from 40 to 25%.

This requirement was not a problem for bankers. So much gold had entered the US banks during the late 1930s, as a result of political and economic instability in Europe, that the Fed had no objection to satisfying the required reserves of gold for decades. However, after the Bretton Woods agreement, which gave the dollar the status of "reserve currency," things began to change. During the decades of 1959 and 1969, the amount of gold in the Federal Reserve decreased considerably. The problem was that, while the gold reserves were decreasing, the bills they issued were rising wildly.

In 1968, the gold reserves held by the Fed compared to the cash in circulation had decreased by 25% as required by law. President Johnson, along with Congress, had no choice but to completely eliminate that restriction and allow the Federal Reserve to issue bills without the need for gold in its vaults.

In February of 1968, the president of the United States, Lyndon Johnson, communicated the following to the Congress:

"The requirement that Federal Reserve notes be backed by gold reserves is not necessary to know what prudent monetary

policy should be: that myth was destroyed long ago. It is not necessary to give value to the dollar, since that value is derived from our productive economy ".

A month later, Congress agreed to the Jonson's request (or bankers?) And the United States stopped backing its Federal Reserve notes with gold. The first obstacle that the Federal Reserve and the other commercial banks had had been eliminated. It should be clarified that if this law had not been modified, either the Federal Reserve would have had to stop printing bills, or it would have had to acquire more gold to back the new bills.

When gold stopped supporting the dollar, the nature of the money changed. The value of banknotes in circulation was no longer derived from a real asset that had an intrinsic value. In other words, the money was no longer *fractional reserve money*, but had completely mutated into a simple *Fiat currency*, which meant that it was only money because the government said it was money. The result of this was the largest credit expansion in history, which transformed the world monetary system and changed our economy forever. The economy stopped being driven by savings and investment, and it was credit and consumption that began to drive economic growth. The creation of credit and accumulation of debt became the vital engine of the new economic system. The credit grew as ever, causing the biggest *boom* in all history. Prosperity increased. House prices rose to historic levels. The actions took off. Millions of jobs were created. Business profits rose to the clouds. The Fiat money supply exploded and the biggest bubble in history was born. The collapse, from then on, was inevitable.

The other obstacle that bankers had to have liquidity reserves to back their deposits was eliminated little by little. The Federal Reserve was created under the obligation that banks should have reserves to guarantee that they had sufficient liquidity to return their deposits to their clients when they requested it. *The Federal Reserve Act* specified that these reserves should be stored in their safes or in the form of deposits in the Federal Reserve. The financial crisis we have today is unleashed because the people and agencies that were responsible for regulating this requirement were reducing over time the volume of reserves that was required to have the financial system, until there came a time when it was an amount so insignificant that they barely restricted the amount of debt that the system could create. In 2007, the reserves were so small that the amount of debt created by the system was much higher than what the world had ever experienced.

NIXON TURNS THE ECONOMY IN A MONOPOLY GAME

The Bretton Woods Agreement worked well for a while, mainly because very few countries actually converted their dollars into gold. The trade balances were settled in US dollars, since it was considered the strongest currency after the Second World War and its status as a "world reserve currency". However, the situation changed drastically.

President Richard Nixon changed the rules of the money because the countries that received payments in dollars began to suspect: the United States was running out of gold and was beginning to become insolvent. The US Department of the Treasury began printing money incessantly to deal with their debts, and this caused the countries that received these dollars to start exchanging them for gold as agreed in the Bretton Woods Agreement, at $ 35 dollars ounce. The US gold reserves began to run out and, little by little, their ability to fulfill the promise with the rest of the world to exchange dollars for gold was evaporating. It was inevitable that this would happen sooner or later: The United States imported more than it exported (that is, it had a trade deficit, something that we will discuss later because it dictates how the economy behaves worldwide) and had to face the Vietnam War, which was a huge expense that it grew more every day. All this happened while importing more and more oil. In short, *the United States was bankrupt because it spent more than it earned.*

French President Charles DeGaulle, seeing that the United States was spending much more than it had in its gold reserves, exchange 300 million

that France had in US dollars for the gold that the United States should have in reserve. Later, the British decided to do the same, and tried to liquidate their dollars in gold. The sum requested would have seriously depleted US gold reserves. The country could not keep its promise with the rest of the world to exchange their dollars for gold because, little by little, the countries began to claim gold in exchange for the dollars and this caused the reserves to disappear. The country was unable to continue backing its notes with gold, so they came to the decision to free the dollar of that metal and prohibit the direct exchange of dollars for gold.

Richard Nixon found a creative way to get out of its debts: abandon the gold standard, print banknotes and convert all currencies into simple Fiat currencies that, from then, would begin to "fluctuate" freely, to compete with each other and to run the risk of speculative attacks by large hedge funds or speculators. On August 15, 1971 is the official date when money stopped being money in the world. That day, the economy of the entire planet changed forever. What the bankers had wanted for centuries had come true: there was no restriction on the amount of money-debt they could print. The party started. On August 15, 1971, Richard Nixon broke the Bretton Woods agreement with the entire world. Without the discipline that gold provides, central banks decided to embark on a process known as "systematic inflation" and turned all employees with fixed income and savers into losers. These people are the biggest losers of the modern economy for several reasons:

- Although employees believe they are working in exchange for money, it is not entirely true. They are paying them with *Fiat currency*, that is, paper money without intrinsic value that is accepted as money because the government says so. Do you think that if money today had value in itself or was backed by gold or silver, the government would force people to use it? The government only forces people to pay their taxes and trade with a Fiat currency because they know that if they do not do it, nobody will accept it as money. Remember: the transition from fractional reserve money to Fiat money (or Fiat currency, to be more exact) requires government intervention.
- Fiat currencies are designed to lose their value: they are worth less every day. Throughout history, all Fiat currencies have returned to their original value: zero.

- As banks have no limit to the amount of money they can print, people's savings each day are worth less. If you save $ 10, but the bank can take them, print $ 90 magically and lend them to someone else, your $ 10 is now worth less because it represents $ 90 in the economy. As there are now more bills in circulation going after the same number of products and services, inflation is inevitable.

- In times of financial uncertainty, all those who accumulated Fiat currencies ended up losing everything.

In the second part of this book I will show you who are the biggest winners in the post-1971 economy and how you can be part of that group.

THE COUNTRIES STARTED TO PLAY WITH MONEY

When the international monetary system of Bretton Woods broke down in 1971, something extraordinary and unthinkable began to happen: the central banks of certain countries began to print Fiat money and to use it to buy the currencies of other countries.

While the Bretton Woods Agreement was in force, the currencies of the countries were fixed directly or indirectly to the dollar. Therefore, nothing was earned by making Fiat money to buy coins from other countries. That changed completely when the system of fixed exchange rates disappeared with the sinking of Bretton Woods.

What did some countries discover? That they could increase their exports if their respective central bank created Fiat money and used it to buy the currencies of their trading partners. When a central bank intervened in this way, the value of the currency that it bought increased and the value of the currency it created was reduced, making the prices of the products of the country that manipulated the currency more competitive in the international market.

How exactly did this process work, where central banks created Fiat money and bought other currencies to increase their foreign exchange reserves? Take China as an example, since it is the country that has the largest amount of currency reserves.

In 2007, before the beginning of the 2008 financial crisis, China's trade surplus with the United States was approximately $ 259 billion. This means that in that year China sold to the United States $ 259 billion dollars more in products and services than the United States sold to China that same year. Obviously, when Chinese companies sell their products to the United States, they charge in dollars. In 2007, these companies took their surplus of $ 259 billion dollars back to China, which is where they were naturally located.

Most businessmen wanted to convert their US dollars into Chinese Yuan. However, if the businessmen had bought Yuan worth $ 259 billion in the currency market without government intervention, the value of the Yuan would have appreciated considerably. The currency markets are governed by supply and demand: more people buying a specific currency pushes the value of that currency upwards, and more people selling a specific currency pushes the value of that currency downwards. If that high sum of dollars were converted into Yuan, the Yuan would have increased a lot in value and the dollar would have suffered a strong devaluation. The increase in the value of the Yuan would have reduced the competitiveness of Chinese exports and, as a result, the growth of exports and China's economic growth would have decreased, taking thousands of jobs with them.

The Chinese government had no intention of slowing growth, so the government ordered the central bank, the People's Bank of China, to buy all the dollars that entered China at a fixed exchange rate so that the Yuan would not appreciate and, precisely, that was what the People's Bank of China did. The central bank created the equivalent of $ 259 billion dollars of Fiat Yuan and used them to buy $ 259 billion dollars, preventing the Yuan from appreciating. In this way, the Chinese companies that took dollars to China could now convert them into Yuan without problems and do with them whatever they wanted. On the other hand, the People's Bank of China ended with $ 259 billion dollars more in their foreign exchange reserves.

Something that should be clear is the following: the Popular Bank of China acquired those dollars with Fiat money that created out of nowhere specifically to fulfill that purpose. This is the way, in which the central banks of some countries accumulate foreign currency reserves, creating Fiat money and using it to buy the currencies of other countries. *The only way for central banks to obtain large amounts of money is to create it.*

Central banks, in 2007, had the equivalent of $ 6.7 billion dollars in foreign exchange reserves. The only possible way for central banks to accumulate such a sum of currency reserves, is through the creation of Fiat money. The creation of money on that scale is unprecedented. All that new money that they have created to manipulate the value of the currency artificially impacts with a huge force in the global economy.

As central banks accumulate foreign currency reserves, whether in dollars, pounds, euros, yen or whatever, they invest them to obtain some return. Of course, a central bank cannot invest reserves in its own economy without converting foreign currencies into national currencies. That is, the Popular Bank of China cannot invest those dollars in its own economy without first exchanging them for Yuan. Naturally, that would push up the value of the national currency, so it would not make sense to buy other currencies in the first place. That is not even an option. The simplest way out is to invest foreign currencies in investment instruments denominated in that currency, and that is what is normally done. For example, the reserves of dollars are invested in treasury bonds that are denominated in dollars, the reserves of euros are invested in bonds denominated in euros, and so on. Government bonds are preferred instruments by central banks because they are considered the safest investment.

Actually, China is the largest foreign holder of US debt. The Popular Bank of China prints Yuan and then uses them to buy dollars in order to keep the Yuan's value low and thus support export-led growth. All this is caused because the United States imports more than it exports. The problem of financing US deficit spending with Fiat money issued by foreign central banks is the power that this gives to the country's competitors. An article in January 2005, in the Asia Times, reveals the following:

"All Beijing has to do is mention the possibility of issuing a sale order for the US bonds it owns. This would devastate the US economy more than a nuclear attack. "

Many are afraid that China will stop buying US debt or suddenly sell the debt it already owns. However, it is almost impossible for this to happen. As we mentioned earlier, if China stopped buying US debt, its economy would collapse, since that would mean that it would have stopped manipulating its currency by buying dollars. If the Popular Bank of China stops printing Yuan and buying dollars to keep the value of the Yuan artificially low, the value of the currency would be doubled by the surplus that this country has with the United States. When Chinese exporters turn their profits by exports of dollars to Yuan, the value of the Yuan would rise so much that exports would become very expensive and China's economy would slow down. The factories would close, unemployment would increase and businessmen would seek to invest in some other country. *If the central bank stops buying US bonds, China would fall apart.*

The other fear is that China sells dollar-denominated assets (bonds and other Treasury debt instruments) worth nearly $ 2 billion dollars, which it is estimated to have in its reserves. If we assume that you find buyers for so many dollars, where would you invest all this new money you would get? There are no debt instruments denominated in euros or in yen or pounds worth more than $ 2 billion for China to buy. Even if China tries to turn some hundreds of billions of dollars into any other currency, this would press so upward on that currency that the issuing country would insist that China stop or, otherwise, bear the consequences. If the Popular Bank of China turned even ¼ of that amount into Yuan, it would be throwing the value of the Yuan into space like a rocket.

China not only cannot sell the reserves of dollars it currently owns, but it must continue to accumulate more dollar reserves every year as long as the trade surplus with the United States continues. If it does not, the huge amount of dollars its exporters earn every year in the United States will push the Yuan up when the exporters take all this money to China and convert it into Yuan. The Chinese government cannot allow this to happen.

SPECULATIVE ATTACKS

With the end of Bretton Woods, the countries were forced to put their currencies to fluctuate in the free market and run the risk of speculative attacks by large hedge funds or speculators. A speculative attack on a currency could devalue it considerably and cause a very high inflation. But what is a speculative attack?

A speculative attack is a practice of attacking stocks or currencies to devalue them, either to obtain a quick profit or to destabilize a company or a country. Using a mechanism called short selling; speculators can make huge profits when the market is collapsing. If the short sales are made on a massive scale, the prices of the stock or the currency in question are forced downwards, allowing it to be acquired later at a very cheap price. Since prices are determined according to supply and demand, when sales orders exceed purchase orders, the price falls. When the price falls, sellers in short repurchase at a lower price and pocket the difference. Nowadays, speculators only have to lower the price of the stock enough to automatically trigger the *orders of maximum loss point and the calls of margin coverage* of the positions of the large hedge funds. When they reach this point, a mountain of sales orders is carried out and the price plummets.

Richard Geist, a market analyst, explains the short sale in simpler terms using the following analogy:

Assume that you borrowed from your neighbor your lawn mower, which your neighbor generously tells you that you can keep for a couple of weeks while he is on vacation. You are thinking about buying a lawn mower anyway, so you have been researching the prices and have seen your neighbor's lawn mower for sale for $ 300, down from 500. While you are mowing your lawn, a person stops and offers to buy the lawn mower he is using for $ 450. You sell the lawn mower, and then go out and buy it, for sale for $ 300, and give it to your neighbor upon your return. Only you have earned $ 150 for the transaction.

It sounds pretty good and very harmless when you use this analogy, right? While in the analogy the neighbor lent his lawn mower, in the real world, short sellers sell shares that do not belong to them and without the authorization of their real owners. In addition, selling the neighbor's lawn mower does not affect the price of them on Wall Street. In the stock market, the prices of the shares fluctuate based on the number of shares for sale. When millions of shares are "sold" without ever having abandoned the ownership of their original owners, these virtual sales can force the price downwards even though there has been no change in the underlying asset to justify the fall. Geist goes on to say the following:

You believe that Amazon's stock is overvalued and that its price will fall. So as a short seller, you take "borrowed" Amazon shares (of which, like the lawn mower, you are not the owner) from a broker and sell them on the market. You borrow and sell 100 Amazon shares at $ 50 per share, producing an income, excluding commissions, of $ 5,000.

His research turns out to be correct and a few weeks later, Amazon's stock is trading at $ 35 per share. So you buy 100 shares of Amazon for $ 3,500 and return the 100 loaned shares to the broker. Finally, you have closed your position and at the same time you have obtained $ 1,500 of profit.

The sale in short is a fraud similar to the fractional reserve system, since the same actions are lent again and again, causing a double claim on them. The analyst David Knight explains it this way:

Short selling is a form of counterfeiting. When a society is founded, a certain number of actions are created. The total value of said company is represented by that fixed number of shares. When an investor buys some of those shares through his stockbroker (who registers them in his name), he leaves them available to someone else to sell them short. Once sold short, there are two investors with the same shares.

The price of the shares is set by market forces, that is, supply and demand. When there is a fixed supply of something, the price adjusts until the demand is balanced. But when the offer is not fixed, as when something is faked, the offer will exceed the demand and the price will fall. The price will continue to fall as long as the supply continues to expand beyond demand. Furthermore, the decline in prices does not behave linearly depending on the expansion of supply. At a certain point, if the supply continues to expand beyond demand, "the floor will fall to the market" and prices will sink.

Like the bankers in antiquity who lent the same gold again and again because they knew that nobody was ever going to claim it, on Wall

Street they lend the same actions again and again without the knowledge of their true owners, in a completely legal way. Wall Street has become the most sophisticated casino in the world, where amateur investors are easy prey for hedge funds and sophisticated investors.

Inflation occurs not only when a government prints money excessively through its central bank, but also when its currency is the victim of a speculative attack. The danger of this was demonstrated in 1992, when George Soros and his giant hedge fund *Quantum Group*, backed by *Citibank* and other powerful speculators, collapsed the currencies of Britain and Italy in a single day. When a currency undergoes a speculative attack, its value decreases considerably. When this happens, of course, prices in the country in question it shoots and cause high inflation. Many Third World countries have suffered speculative attacks that caused heavy domestic inflation, which has been mistakenly attributed to their respective governments and central banks for bad monetary policy.

THE TRUE WORLD CRISIS: DERIVATIVES

Nuclear weapons are not the biggest threat in our world. A third world war is not the greatest threat in our world. A terrorist attack in Washington, Moscow, London or Beijing is not the biggest threat to our world. Financial derivatives are the biggest threat we currently have and the real ones responsible for the 2008 financial crisis.

But what is a financial derivative? In simple terms, derivatives are financial instruments whose price and value are derived from the value of the assets that support them. An example is mortgages:

mortgages are derivatives whose value is derived from real estate. Let's start by explaining them with simple definitions. Let's say you have $ 100 and you want to get a return on this money. A friend needs just that amount, so you decide to make a loan for your 100 dollars a year with an interest of 10%. At the end of the year, you will get your 100 dollars back plus a profit of 10 dollars representing the interest. You just created a financial derivative. The $ 10 profit is a derivative of the initial $ 100. This is a derivative of the first level, and so far, everything is going quite well.

Now let's suppose that your friend comes to you to propose the same business, but you do not have the 100 dollars. You see an opportunity that you cannot let go and, as a businessman that you are, you know that you do not need to have money to make money. Immediately you see the business opportunity, go with your parents and ask them for 100 dollars loaned for a year at 5% interest. Your parents accept your terms immediately, and you take those 100 dollars and lend them to your friend at 10% interest for a year. After one year, your friend will return you 110 dollars, of which 105 are used to pay the debt with your parents plus interest, and the remaining 5 are your profit. In this way, you have just made money without having money, all thanks to the fact that you created a *derivative of a derivative*, that is, a derivative of the second level.

The banks take the show to a much more sophisticated level: they create a *derivative of a derivative of a derivative*, that is, a derivative of the third level, all thanks to the system of the fractional reserve that we have already explained in this book. The problem is that this Ponzi scheme was provided many more steroids during the crisis, taking financial derivatives to levels never seen before.

It all started with *securitization*, which changed the role of banks' intermediaries, and with the repeal of the Glass-Steagall Act, which prohibited deposit banks from engaging in speculative activities and allowed investment banks to merge with the deposit banks. Previously, when a bank granted a mortgage, it retained it and obtained interest income while the mortgage was in effect. The same thing happened with credit cards. The banks kept their asset portfolios and made profits for the interest they received. With the securitization, however, the bank can download its portfolio of assets by selling it to interested investors through a special partnership (*Special Purpose Vehicles*, or SPV, which is the most used). For example, a bank has a mortgage loan portfolio, but instead of keeping it, it sells it to the SPV. If the bank has 100,000 mortgage loans, they can be purchased by the SPV. This, in turn, issues securities to finance the purchase. In the case of mortgages, these securities are known as MBS (*Mortgage-backed securities*); When it comes to other types of loans (credit cards, car financing, etc.) the bank can also build packages, and the SPV issues securities known as ABS (*Asset-backed securities*). Both MBS and ABS are very attractive to investors since they yield higher interest than government or corporate securities. In the seven years prior to the outbreak of the financial crisis, the US securitization market went from an issuance of less than $ 500,000 million, to more than $ 2 billion in 2006; in 2007, the stock of MBS had a value of about $ 5.8 trillion dollars.

Therefore, when a bank gives you a loan to buy a home, it rarely keeps the credit; instead, it is sold to Wall Street or an investment bank, where, in turn, they convert it into a package together with other mortgage loans, transforming it into an MBS, or a mortgage backed guarantee. Once converted into an MBS, it is sold to investors around the world.

There were also other derivatives, apart from the MBS and ABS, which joined the party and inflated the bubble more. One of the most important were the *Credit-default swaps*, or CDS, which consist, in essence, in contracts that grant insurance against "default" or defaults. To understand it better, suppose that A is an insurance company that sells protection against default to B, which is an issuer of mortgage securities. A CDS contract is then established between A and B, by which A receives a part of the interest flow that yields the security (that part of the yield is supposed to represent the risk), in exchange for the commitment to respond for the value of the security and the interest due, in case the mortgage debtor default. Many companies embarked on this business of selling protection. In mid-2008 AIG, the largest insurance company in the world, owned CDS linked to the mortgage market for $ 450,000 million dollars. When the mortgage debtors stopped paying, AIG had no way to cover so many defaults at the same time; the same thing happened with other financial and insurance companies. But at the time of the credit *boom*, the CDS allowed giving the impression that the insured MBS were free of risk, which caused large institutional investors (pension funds, university funds, etc.) that are prohibited by law from investing in risky portfolios; they will be encouraged and enter the "risk free MBS" casino.

The party did not stop there. The creation of new derivatives, *Collateralized* debt, or CDO, which mean *Collateralized Debt Obligations*, was added to the CDS. These were issued with the support of MBS mortgage securities or other types of securities. In other words, they were packages that were made with packages of titles. What was the meaning of the CDO? They were sold under the assumption that this was more diversified risk, because the characteristic of the CDO is that they segmented the credit according to different degrees of risk. Thus, it is established that those investors who buy the CDO stretch called *equity*, bear the first losses, in case the debtors fail to comply, until they reach 3% of the total portfolio of underlying securities. The next stretch, known as *mezzanine*, absorbs up to 10% of losses; and the *senior* stretches, which were considered to be very low risk, the following losses. Those who assume more risk, of course, receive more interest.

While these complex financial derivatives began to take hold, the rating agencies also did their part to boost the credit *boom*. The rating agencies charge to inform investors how much risk they are assuming when purchasing a title. And the more titles they qualify, the more money they earn. Therefore, these companies of "experts" were very interested in putting good grades on the titles they received. Here there was a confluence of interests: those who sold the securities were interested in the rating agencies judging that there was no risk and the rating agencies, in turn, were very willing to look the other way, because the more volume of papers they qualified, the higher they were his earnings. And on the other hand, the institutional investors were also interested in the ratings being good, since they wanted eagerly to enter the business that seemed to be a wheel of endless fortune. The volumes that qualified these agencies were gigantic. For example, between 2002 and 2006, Moody's (a risk rating company) obtained more than $ 3,000 million for rating securities based on mortgage loans. The rating agencies rate these securities as follows: AAAs are the safest of all and are qualified for those mortgage loans granted to people with a very good credit rating and an impeccable record; BBBs are the next safest, although they do not have the same quality as AAAs; the following are so risky that rating agencies do not bother or name, and are mortgage loans commonly known as *subprime*. Every time you hear the word subprime, think trash. Subprime borrowers are those who do not have the economic capacity to cope with their debts, and it is expected that, barring a miracle, they will default at some point in the future. One of the triggers of the crisis is that risk rating agencies rated subprime loans as AAA, deceiving investors and making them think that they were buying meat of the best quality, when what they were really acquiring was manure.

Attracted by the smell of easy money, many investment banks, commercial banks, and other financial institutions got into business. Again, a special entity was created, which issued the CDOs, and with the received, it bought the MBS (or the ABS). The CDO issuers earned by the commissions and the management of the titles. Hence his interest in placing huge volumes. The problem was that *nobody knew with certainty how much risk these instruments contained.* And the casino went out of control when CDOs began to be *squared*, that is, new CDOs backed by CDO were issued. They were packets of packages of titles. And, of course, those who called themselves "experts" still rated them with the best scores. In addition, many banks acquired the *mezzanine*, or *senior* stretches. Of being almost negligible at the beginning of the 2000s, the issuance of CDO reached in 2006 the almost $ 400 billion dollars. The table was set for a worldwide disaster.

The reason why the collapse of real estate in the United States paralyzed the world economy was by derivatives, among them, the MBS. The derivatives are responsible for the foreclosures in San

Francisco causing a town in Greece to go bankrupt. Its tentacles are spread throughout all countries. One of the biggest problems is that the derivatives market is not regulated. Derivatives are not subject to the standards and regulations of an official institution. They are monsters so big that they make the other markets look like dwarfs at their side. It is estimated that the derivatives market is equivalent to ten times the global PIB. For this reason, Warren Buffett says the following: "*Derivatives are weapons of mass destruction.*"

It should be remembered and be very clear that the derivatives are not active. They are only bets on what will happen to an asset. And to return the most interesting bet, very little "real" money is used. Most of the money used in these bets is borrowed from banks that create it on a computer screen at the same time the loan is made. As these private bets are not communicated or regulated, nobody knows exactly how much money is at stake in them. It is said that they were designed purposely complicated so that no one understands them. The language that is used to understand derivatives is confusing and deceptive on purpose, however, its consequences affect us all. The derivatives are like two people throwing a coin into the air for a trillion dollars, and then someone finds himself owing a billion dollars that never existed.

In a report by the Department of the Currency in 2006, it was found that more than 97% of the financial derivatives held by banks were concentrated in five of them, of which J.P. Morgan Chase and Citibank. The article continues saying: *"The biggest player of derivatives, J.P. Morgan Chase, is comprised in a part of up to $ 57 billion dollars in hypothetical value of derivatives. His total credit exposure reaches $ 660 billion, an amazing 748% of the bank's risk-based capital. In other words, for every dollar of its net value, J.P.*

Morgan Chase is risking $ 7.48 in derivatives. All that is needed is that 13.3% of its derivatives go badly and the capital of J.P. Morgan would be erased, it would disappear. Citibank is not far behind: with 4.24 dollars in risk for every dollar of capital. "With that level of leverage and risk handled by some of the most powerful banks in the world, it is easy to reach the following conclusion*: if only one of these banks fails, it takes the economy of the entire world with it.* The public does not have the slightest idea that the world's financial system could be frozen one day to another if a small percentage of the derivatives began to fail. J.P. Morgan Chase and Citibank belong to the financial empires of Morgan and Rockefeller, two of the banking consortia that were present at the meeting of Jekyll Island, when the birth of the Federal Reserve was discussed. They can keep betting on these complex financial instruments with complete peace of mind, as they belong to the select club called "too big to fail".

When ordinary citizens bet their money, they go to casinos or buy lottery tickets. However, when bankers bet, they use the money of others; they buy dangerous bets on Wall Street called derivatives, *make bets on their bets*, and are covered against all kinds of losses by taxpayers. I wonder what these guys smoked. The world would be much better if we all bet in Las Vegas instead of allowing a handful of bankers to bet on Wall Street.

I hate to be the one who has to tell you this, but if you are the average person who has a job, works hard, saves money and invests in a pension plan, then the financial system is against you and will make you poorer every day. The winners are those who manage the money printing and those who know how to borrow that money to acquire legitimate assets. In the second part I will show you how you can become a winner in this financial system.

THE BUBBLE BURSTS

The economy is like a bicycle: either it advances or it falls. That was reflected in the crisis of 2008. When the bubble stopped inflating, collapsed; when the economy stopped growing, collapsed; when credit ceased to expand, collapsed; when the speculators stopped buying, collapsed; when the Fed raised interest rates, collapsed; when real estate stopped rising in price, collapsed. As in any Ponzi fraud, the bubble must keep growing or inevitably burst. The system climbed to the top and, once at the top, the only possible destination was the fall. And that was exactly what happened. The disaster was created because the Federal Reserve kept interest rates too low for too long, to stimulate the economy after the Internet bubble at the beginning of the 21st century. These very low interest rates caused a huge wave of money and cheap credit, which caused inflation and speculation and caused housing prices to rise mainly to historical levels. Since the credit was so cheap and easy to obtain, the banks were quick to grant loans to any bum who passed by on the street, with the only condition that he had to be well groomed. It did not matter if the bum had a job, stable income, minimal credit rating or anything else. Nobody noticed that, and if a bank rejected him, then the bank on the next corner would accept him. Afterwards, the banks took all these mortgages, sold them to Wall Street, and the financial geniuses bundled the insurance and subprime loans (toxic loans), transformed them into MBS (mortgage backed collateral) and sold it to the investors of the entire world. When the Federal Reserve lowers interest rates, it becomes cheap for banks to borrow money. Banks start asking the Fed for money and then look for people with fixed incomes who can acquire debts and pay them. The drawback for bankers came when people who could acquire a mortgage and have their own house was over. It was evident that this would happen, after all, there are only a certain number of people who meet the requirements to access these loans. At this point, banks began to lower their standards and become very careless with the requirements to grant loans. The game began to become dangerous and ridiculous when people who in normal situations would never have agreed to a loan, now not only had their own house, but condominiums and vacation homes. People suddenly felt enriched by the increase in the value of their homes, and began to use them as cash machines. If a person bought a house for $ 300,000, and after one year the property was worth $ 350,000, the bank gave him these $ 50,000 extra dollars through a refinance. Under the erroneous notion that real estate was always going to rise in price, people began to refinance their homes to pay off credit card debts, go on vacation, buy a television or pay the down payment for another home. Everything would continue to go well if properties continued to rise in price, but if in the future they could not refinance because interest rates had gone up or real estate had stagnated, they would be fried. And evidently, they ended up fried.

After a while, something happened that nobody was waiting for: the expected adjustments to the rates arrived. Most buyers fell into the trap of these "bait" rates, which allow low-income people to pay a very low initial fee and take on a mortgage where interest rates and monthly payments fluctuate with market conditions. The owners who agreed to this agreement (which was a very high percentage) were betting that either their income would increase to cover the overcharge in payments, or that the real estate market would continue rising, allowing them to sell their home with a gain before the adjustments to the rates came.

Subprime loans were the first to enter into default. The adjustments to the rates annihilated these people and the mortgages were executed. However, something very interesting happened with the people who could still make the payments. When subprime borrowers stopped paying their loans, a wave of foreclosures devalued the real estate market and the price of homes sank. A person who had bought a house for $ 400,000 and had the resources to pay the mortgage, now faced a scenario where his house was worth $ 250,000, but his mortgage was kept intact by the purchase value of the property, that is, $ 400,000 dollars. This person began to question himself: "Why am I going to continue paying a $ 400,000 mortgage when the house is now worth only $ 250,000? I'm not that stupid. "And that's how the AAA and BBB loans went into default. When the *prime* loans also began to fail, a rash of record highs caused the MBS to fail, along with all the derivatives that were on the table: CDS and CDO mainly. The problem with these derivatives is that nobody knew with certainty who could be at the end of the chain. It could be a corporation in Switzerland that was bankrupt and could not pay its debts and, in that case, there was a domino effect in which each of the parties has problems to pay the next.

Cheap credit could not sustain the bubble indefinitely. It is a mistake to think that credit can prolong accumulation indefinitely, or even for decades. If a worker takes out a real estate loan, he must pay the agreed fees, or face fines and the risk of losing his home. To comply, he will have to generate value (mainly from your salary or labor). If for some reason this does not happen, it will default. If the creditor executes the mortgage, the realization of the value of the home will depend on market conditions. In the case that many mortgage debtors enter into default, the collapse of prices and values will be inevitable. Then there is no credit injection that saves the capitalist system from the losses; *new credit flows may postpone the outbreak, but they do not prevent it, since credit, by itself, in the long or medium term, does not have the capacity to generate new purchasing power.* For this reason, those in charge of monetary policy were forced to become very creative so that the casino would keep working.

QUANTITATIVE EASING

The domino effect of the crisis was devastating: the borrowers stopped paying their mortgages; therefore the MBS lost all their value because they are derivatives that depend on the value of the mortgages; the CDS and CDO collapsed because they are derivatives from MBS, causing the bankruptcy of several investment banks, states, investment funds and financial institutions; insurers could not cope with the huge amount of defaults, and could not fulfill their obligations; the system was about to collapse, the cash machines were about to stop withdrawing money, banks were about to close their doors, people were saying goodbye to their pension, workers were being fired, and the government was facing a crisis that threatened to destroy civilization as we know it. The plan that was on the desk of the managers was clear: it had to rescue the people who had caused the crisis in the first place, and the taxpayers, and their children, and the children of their children, were going to pay this ransom with taxes and inflation. The bankers had the economy hostage, and if they went bankrupt, so would we. The printers were ready to start working, this time, at levels never before seen.

What have central banks and governments done since the global financial crisis of 2008? Print more Fiat money, increase indebtedness, lower interest rates and keep the economy afloat artificially. Let's imagine that a ship is at sea, sinking, and that the captain in charge and the crew are desperate evacuating the water to keep it afloat. Now, instead of a large wooden boat, imagine a pneumatic raft inflated with debt, which has numerous holes and is in danger of debt to escape through them. The bankers and politicians in charge of the economy are desperately inflating the raft with debt so that it does not continue sinking. That boat, of course, is the world economy. All humanity lives in it. There are no lifeguards. If the boat sinks, we all sink with it. That harsh reality is what dictates and will continue to dictate monetary policy. The hope that the managers rescue us every day decreases more. They cannot fix the boat, the only thing they can do is postpone the sinking. They will continue inflating with debt the raft in which we are all until they run out of strength and cannot inject more debt. They are lost at sea and do not know what else they can do.

The global financial crisis that began in 2008 was the consequence of a badly regulated banking system where power was concentrated in the hands of a few. Things have not changed much today.

Since the crisis, the G7 central banks have injected money into markets and private banks through a very unconventional process called *Quantitative Easing* (QE). Quantitative Easing is an extremely complex term that very few people really understand. Its name tries to deceive the public of what it really means. The QE implies that a central bank manufactures electronic money and then injects it into banks and financial markets in exchange for the purchase of bonds or shares. The result of applying this process is to raise the money supply within the financial system, reduce interest rates (or the cost of borrowing, disproportionately in favor of banks and larger corporations) and boost the value of those bonds or shares. All this cycle that takes place behind the scenes causes the cost of money to become abnormally cheap and artificially keep the system on its feet.

Speculation broke out as a result of this abundant cheap capital, in the same way that a global casino would be disturbed if everyone bet with another person's money. The problem is that this QE policy did not make bank loans grow, nor did wages increase, nor did the prosperity of most people improve. On the contrary, central banks created bubbles through their artificial stimulation. When these bubbles explode, the fragile financial system and the underlying economic world could be engulfed in depression. For this reason, central banks are conspiring together and acting in sync.

Almost ten years after the crisis began, the six major banks in the United States, made up of J.P. Morgan Chase, Citigroup, Wells Fargo, Bank of America, Goldman Sachs and Morgan Stanley collectively hold 48% more deposits, 87% more active and three times more money than they had before the crisis. The Federal Reserve allowed the largest Wall Street banks to double the risk that wiped out the system in 2008.

Since the crisis erupted, banks and markets have been subsidized by central banks and their "quantitative policies" of easy money. Instead of fixing the economy with authentic, sustained and long-term growth, central banks provide artificial money globally. The most chilling thing about this whole process, however, is that central banks have no exit strategy for their policies.

Why did the central bankers decide to implement and make several rounds of "Quantitative Easing"? The people in charge of the financial system realized that the simple fact of lowering interest rates in their countries was no longer effective if they did not apply a Quantitative Easing. They had to apply policies that they had never implemented before if they wanted to continue playing Monopoly. They had to conspire together for these measures to be applied worldwide and everyone was following the same toxic recipe. These people invented and deposited cash in their respective banking systems, and surely they will do it as many times as necessary in order to maintain the system standing up.

One of the biggest problems of having an economic system based on so much money Fiat created from out of nowhere, is that when bankers stop creating it, the system goes into shock: markets collapse, credit freezes and the economy stops. The Great Depression is an example of this. Years of cheap capital created a huge bubble that, to stop it, the bankers who had started it had to stop injecting Fiat money into the economy. When they adopted this measure, the system imploded. If the Fed currently raises interest rates too high or too fast, it can cause a global collapse. It does not matter where you look at the problem that the financial system is facing today: everywhere, you will find that collapse is inevitable. The question is not whether it will happen or not, but when it will happen. The pneumatic raft on which we are all assembled has too many holes. Its shipwreck is inevitable.

THE SECRET BANKRUPTCY OF THE BANKS

After having read this far and having understood what we have discussed in the previous chapters, you may ask yourself: If banks can create money out of nowhere and without any restriction, why are they in trouble? How is it possible for some to declare bankruptcy if they have the ability to print money at will? Why does not a bank with toxic loans in their books just not cancel them and continue as usual?

The important fact, which we have already made clear throughout this book and that we must keep in mind, is that all the events of the banks and the financial system start from the fact that all the money has been created from out of nowhere through the process to grant loans. Therefore, when the loans begin to fail, the bank does not lose much in tangible value, but it is obliged to show in its books a reduction in assets without a corresponding reduction in liabilities. The reduction of assets is evident, since the borrower will no longer pay the respective interest. But what must be understood is that the liabilities cannot be reduced, since that money is still owed to the depositor. Remember that when a bank lends money, it is creating an asset (because the borrower is assumed to pay it back with their respective interests) and a liability (because that loan becomes a deposit, and a deposit is an obligation that has the bank to return the money when required), so their books are balanced: an asset supports a liability. Now, when you make a bad loan and the borrower cannot even pay the interest, the bank's assets decrease, but the liability remains intact. If the toxic loans exceed the size of the assets, the bank technically becomes insolvent and must close its doors.

Bankers have learned these lessons throughout their history, and the "banking panics" have made them realize that they need someone to rescue them from their own stupidity. They have devised several practical ways to survive and avoid bankruptcy, no matter how stupid they are, how risky are the loans they give or the compromised positions in which they find themselves.

- Roll Over: The first way they devised to survive is to avoid amortizing large and toxic loans and, if possible, at least continue to receive interest from them. To achieve this, the dangerous loans are applied a "roll over" and an increase in size. What this means, in a nutshell, is that they refinance the debt, giving the borrower new money to continue paying interest and have something extra to spend on what they want. The problem of toxic debt has not been resolved for the bank, it has only been postponed and worsened because the leverage of the borrower has increased.

- Congress: The banking cartel must ensure that the government guarantees the payment of bad loans in case they fail in the future. To achieve this, Congress must be convinced that if they do not, the result will be the collapse of the economy. If Congress falls into the trap (and will surely do so), the burden of all the bad loans that the bank made is transferred to the taxpayers. This happened recently in the United States, where Congress gave the key to the Treasury Department to Wall Street banks to take $ 700 billion of taxpayers' money. This did not save the depositors from losing their savings or their pensions or granting new loans to small businesses, but it went directly to the pocket of the owners of the banks.

- Bank Deposit Insurance: If the assistance from Congress is not enough and fails, the bank resorts to using the FDIC (Bank Deposit Insurance) to pay depositors and avoid insolvency. The problem is that the FDIC does not have the capacity to insure all the existing deposits.

- Federal Reserve: When these funds run out (since the FDIC does not insure 100% of the deposits), the balance is provided by the Federal Reserve, which enters the game as a "lender of last resort", creating all the debt and the money that the system requires. All this money Fiat created out of nowhere floods the economy, giving the impression of an increase in prices when, really, it is money that is losing its value and is being devalued.
The help provided by the government and the central bank is only given to the banks belonging to the select club called "very big to fail". Small banks that do not have political influence, therefore, if they must assume the consequences of the free market and close their doors if they become insolvent.

It does not matter what happens, in the end, the total cost of the rescue will be borne by the taxpayers, either with taxes directly or with the invisible tax called inflation. All this leads us to analyze the following.

MORAL RISK

If a person acquires a total insurance against any damage or theft of their vehicle, they will not have any incentive to take care of it or to be cautious, since it does not matter how stupid it is or how careless it is, it is 100% covered.

Likewise, banks have acquired total insurance against any type of disaster that occurs in the economy, either directly caused by them or by someone else. Unless a revolution occurs where taxpayers refuse to continue supporting these banks or the system implodes completely, large banks will remain immune to the free market.

Small banks can fail and break, but great banks, no matter how incompetent or fraudulent they are, are insured for being "too big to fail". You and I can break, but the bank cannot, because the Global Monopoly game must continue. We must all pay attention to the Monopoly rule that warns us this:

"The bank never breaks, if it run out of money, it can create all the money you need just by printing it on any ordinary paper."

HOW WILL THE CRISIS EVOLVE IN THE FUTURE?

What will happen in the future? What will happen to the world economy? Will this economy based on Fiat money survive? Will the money have value or become trash? Can banks continue playing

Monopoly? The answer to all this depends on the debt: it depends on whether the debt contracts or expands.

Something that must be understood is that in this new global financial system, credit (or debt) is what determines whether we will live through a period of expansion or contraction. If the debt increases, the expansion will begin. The problem of an expansion sustained by debt and low interest rates, is that unless banks and governments continue to inject more and more debt into the bubble, it will eventually burst when the debt is reversed or the system cannot absorb more credit. The house of cards, sooner or later, will collapse. There is no doubt about that. The question is: when it collapses, will it be because of the excess debt (hyperinflation) or because of the contraction and the shortage of debt (deflation)? As the debt is the new money, a destruction of it would cause a great contraction of the money supply, which would lead to a depression like the one of 1929.

One thing is for sure: the crisis will come. If the debt is contracted, the depression will be by deflation, like 1929. If the debt expands without control, it is possible that the economy inflates in such a way that we face a depression due to hyperinflation, like the one that Germany lived in. previous century or the one Venezuela currently lives. If we analyze the policies of central banks and governments in response to the crisis, the conclusion is that they will print all the money necessary to prevent the economy from entering into a depression. If they exceed and kill the dollar, we will enter a period of hyperinflation. The second part of this book will teach you to prepare for this scenario with the best investment vehicle that exists: real estate.

In summary, this is the scenario we face today:

- Never before in history has money been so cheap for so long.
- Never before in history have certain elite central banks attempted to control all others.
- Never before in history have central banks tried and managed to dominate the world monetarily and economically.
- Never before in history had a great depression been postponed keeping the system artificially standing for so long.

The hard truth is that we are all part of this now. The artificial money bubble has enveloped us all and taken the world economy hostage. Except continue printing money, there is no plan b in case of another crisis. Like Dr. Frankenstein, bankers have created something with implications beyond their own understanding. The Jekyll Island monster has grown a lot and has become very powerful. Now it is present on all continents and forces the masses to serve it, feed it, obey it and worship it. He has become our Master and manages the fate of our world behind the scenes.

SUMMARY:

- The collapse of 1929 was the largest bank stampede in history.
- The Federal Reserve assisted England by keeping interest rates low and preventing gold from escaping to the United States. These low interest rates caused a bubble in the United States and later a depression that lasted more than a decade.
- Since all the money in existence comes from the act of borrowing, when the Federal Reserve raises interest rates, reserves decrease, loans become more expensive and money in circulation is scarce.
- When the Fed purchases debt, the money supply expands, and when the Fed sells debt, the money supply contracts.
- In a financial crisis, wealth is not destroyed, it simply transfers.
- In general, the intrinsic value of assets does not change, its price is altered by economic conditions and speculators. This means that when the real estate market collapses, it is not because the real estate is no longer profitable or does not generate cash flow; it simply means that speculators and amateur investors inflated it excessively with the help of the bankers and believed that they could get rich quickly by "buying cheap and selling expensive". Legitimate investors (those who invest in cash flow) take advantage of collapses to buy assets at half price.
- The depression of 1929 was a depression by deflation, which means the following: as all the money in circulation was born through the act of borrowing, when the interest rates went up,

the loans failed and the delinquency increased, the money began to disappear.

- In 1929 the Federal Reserve did not print money to keep the economy afloat, and in 2008 it did. That is why in 1929 the depression was due to deflation and currently the Federal Reserve is following the path of hyperinflation.

- The Bretton Woods Agreement was concluded in 1944, at the end of the Second World War, and gave birth to the International Monetary Fund, the World Bank and the new world reserve currency, the US dollar.

- In February 1968, the president of the United States, Lyndon Johnson, with the approval of Congress, stipulated that the Federal Reserve did not have to continue to have gold to back its tickets. The nature of money changed completely and credit grew to imagined levels. The dollar had become a simple *Fiat currency*, which meant that it was only money because the government said it was.

- On August 15, 1971 Richard Nixon broke the Bretton Woods Agreement and stopped exchanging dollars for gold. That day, the economy of the entire planet changed forever. The bankers began to live their dreams: there was no restriction on the amount of money-debt they could print.

- All employees with fixed incomes and savers became losers when the currencies stopped being backed by gold because the money they work for each day is worth less.

- With the end of Bretton Woods, the central banks of certain countries began to print Fiat money and to use it to buy the currencies of other countries. This devalued the currency that they manipulated and appreciated the currency they acquired.

In this way they stimulated exports by making them more competitive in the global market.

- Central banks, in 2007, had the equivalent of $ 6.7 billion in foreign exchange reserves. The only possible way for central banks to accumulate such a sum of currency reserves is through the creation of Fiat money. The creation of money on that scale is unprecedented.

- A speculative attack is a practice of attacking stocks or currencies to devalue them, either to obtain a quick profit or to destabilize a company or a country, through an action known as "short sale".

- A speculative attack on a currency could devalue it considerably and cause a very high inflation.

- Inflation occurs not only when a government prints money excessively through its central bank, but also when its currency is the victim of a speculative attack.

- Financial derivatives are the biggest threat we currently have and the real ones responsible for the 2008 financial crisis.

- Derivatives are financial instruments whose price and value are derived from the value of the assets that support them. The derivatives are not assets. They are only bets on what will happen to an asset. And to return the most interesting bet, very little "real" money is used. Most of the money used in these bets is borrowed from banks that create it on a computer screen at the same time the loan is made.

- The economy is like a bicycle: either it advances or it falls.

- "Quantitative Easing" (QE) is an extremely complex term that very few people really understand. Its name tries to deceive the public of what it really means. The QE implies that a central bank manufactures electronic money and then injects it into banks and financial markets in exchange for the purchase of bonds or shares. The result of applying this process is to raise the money supply within the financial system, reduce interest rates and boost the value of those bonds or stocks. This whole cycle that takes place behind the scenes causes the cost of money to become abnormally cheap and artificially keep the system on its feet. Several rounds of QE have been needed by the most powerful central banks in the world so that the great depression that we should have experienced in 2008 was postponed.

- One of the biggest problems of having an economic system based on so much Fiat money created out of nowhere, is that when the bankers stop creating it, the system goes into shock.

- All the events of the banks and the financial system start from the fact that all the money has been created from out of nowhere through the process of granting loans.

- When a bank lends money, it is creating an asset (because the borrower is assumed to pay it back with their respective interests) and a liability (because that loan becomes a deposit, and a deposit is an obligation that the bank to return the money when required), so your books are balanced: an asset supports a liability. Now, when you make a bad loan and the borrower cannot even pay the interest, the bank's assets decrease, but the liability remains intact. If the toxic loans exceed the size of the assets, the bank technically becomes insolvent and must close its doors.

- When we go to the bank to ask for a loan, in reality the bank does not lend us the money from their deposits. Instead of that, at the moment the pen touches that mortgage, loan document or credit card receipt signed by us, the bank is creating that money through the accounting record. In other words, we created that money because the bank could not do it without our signature. We create the money and then the bank charges us interest on it. But when a property is going to be auctioned, when someone cannot continue paying their loans or declares bankruptcy, that money simply disappears. Therefore, when the credit or the debt has some problem, the money supply contracts and inflation is declared.

- The help provided by the government and the central bank is only provided to the banks that belong to the select club called "very big to fail". Small banks that do not have political influence, therefore, if they must assume the consequences of the free market and close their doors if they become insolvent.

- What will happen in the future? The answer to all this depends on the debt: it depends on whether the debt contracts or expands.

- In this new global financial system, credit (or debt) determines whether we will live through a period of expansion or contraction. In other words: the policies that the central banks decide are the ones that have the last word on our financial future. The presidents have very little power to influence the decision of these bankers. Even Donald Trump himself referred to the matter: *"The only problem of the economy of the United States is the Federal Reserve."*

Chapter 5

Petrodollars and the Global Empire

"The world is governed by characters very different from those imagined by those who are not behind the scenes."

–Benjamin Disraeli, British Prime Minister from 1868 to 1880

Why does the dollar have so much weight in the world? Why does Washington worry and intervene when some countries stop negotiating with dollars? Why is the dollar so valuable, if it is already clear in the previous chapters that it is simply a piece of paper? If all currencies are paper only, why does the dollar stand out from the other currencies?

After Nixon definitively abandoned gold in 1971, the dollar became a simple Fiat currency. If the United States wanted to continue dominating the empire it had developed up to that moment, it should look for something that would give the dollar a unique value and force other countries to accept it without questions. President Nixon, in his eagerness to keep intact the American monopoly in the world, traveled to Saudi Arabia and spoke with the King to negotiate an agreement that would change the economy of the entire world. Nixon offered him all the weapons and security he needed and, in return, Saudi Arabia and the OPEC countries (the Organization of Petroleum Exporting Countries) would commit to trading oil only in US dollars. I think we all know what would have happened if Saudi Arabia refused to accept that agreement.

The US agreement with the royal family of Saudi Arabia, the biggest oil producer in OPEC included a commitment on the part of OPEC to sell the oil only in US dollars and, in exchange, Saudi Arabia would receive arms and the House Saud would have the protection of the United States to stay in power. The agreement basically consisted of giving them money for protection and making sure that the House of Saud would not follow the same path as Iran.

The US dollar, once the most valuable in the world for its exchange in gold, was now "backed" by oil. The countries were now obliged to acquire newly printed monopoly notes from the Federal Reserve to buy this essential resource. This caused countries that imported oil worldwide to be forced to export goods, in order to obtain dollars and pay their new and expensive oil import accounts.

PETRODOLLARS SPREAD THROUGH THE WORLD

In the 1970s, the price of oil quadrupled, and OPEC countries were suddenly flooded with US dollars. This new wave of *petrodollars* needed to find a safe home, so they went to banks in London and New York and, once there, bankers recycled them and made loans to third world countries. These loans granted by the commercial banks were the same as the loans we mentioned earlier and, therefore, did not arise from the money they had in deposits for their clients, but were made with money newly created for this purpose. The deposits acted only as "reserves" for the loans created from out of nowhere through the fractional reserve system. This act of magic allowed the bankers to multiply many times the petrodollars of the Arab sheiks and to indebt all the naive countries that accepted them.

Once the petrodollars came to the biggest banks in London, the bankers there began to look for a new home. The countries of Latin America requested all this money with great pleasure, and in the late 1970s and early 1980s, the Latin American economy had transformed into a huge bubble that later exploded, producing a credit crisis in many countries. The petrodollars had done their job, and then they migrated to Japan to produce again a bubble that finally exploded in 1989. Then that *hot money* flowed into Mexico, causing the Mexican peso crisis of 1994 and, later, the Asian crisis of 1997 and that of the ruble in Russia in 1998.

When these petrodollars flowed to the United States again, Fannie Mae and Freddie Mac (the two biggest companies that guaranteed mortgages in the United States), along with the biggest banks in the country, accepted this money, made *subprime* loans, produced derivatives of these loans, then they derived derivatives of those loans until, finally, in 2008, the economy of the United States collapsed and took much of the world with them. The petrodollars then went to countries that were once rich and powerful, such as Portugal, Ireland, Italy, Greece and Spain (which are commonly known as PIIGS), and turned them into lost cases by destroying their economies that may not be they will recover in a long time.

Why did these petrodollars cause so much volatility and bubbles where they went? When banks obtain a lot of money in the form of deposits, their reserves increase and, subsequently, their loans increase. When banks lend, prices go up. When prices rise, banks lend more and more and more ... until the economy can no longer withstand more indebtedness. People borrow as much as they can, until a day comes when they can no longer return the money and, then, the money warms up they go in search of a new home to do it all over again. Murray Rothbard explained this phenomenon magnificently:

"The expansion of bank credit sets in motion the economic cycle in all its phases: the inflationary expansion, characterized by an expansion of the money supply and by bad investments; the crisis, which comes when the expansion of credit ceases and bad investments are evident; and the recovery of the depression, the necessary adjustment process by which the economy returns to the most efficient ways of satisfying the desires of the consumers ".

AMERICAN HYPERINFLATION

The reason why the United States is such a "rich" country today is because it is in the unique position of having its currency accepted as a world reserve currency. This means that the US dollar is the most accepted currency as a means of international trade, which gives it a unique advantage. If any other country had this advantage, it would also be a rich country today. This advantage allows the United States to create money from out of nowhere to trade internationally, and the other countries have no choice but to accept it. This explains why the trade deficit is out of control in the United States and does not seem to worry anyone in charge. While this hegemony of the dollar continues, the United States will be able to continue spending more than it earns and will not know the consequences of its irresponsible acts. As long as the other countries follow the game, the Federal Reserve will create all the toy money that is necessary.

The United States has done an incredible feat that is unprecedented: it has been able to finance its trade deficit with Fiat money printed by themselves. Although, in reality, the United States is not affected by its trade deficit in the least. In fact, it is the biggest beneficiary of all, while its business partners are the victims of the game. The United States gets the cars, televisions and other goods of the countries, while they get the Monopoly money. However, there is a latent danger known to the White House and the Federal Reserve Board. As long as the dollar remains at the top as a trading currency, the United States will be able to continue with the party spending more than it earns. But when the day arrives (and it will arrive), when the dollar collapses and the countries and commercial partners do not accept it anymore, the free ride will end. When this happens, hundreds of billions of dollars that are now resting abroad will quickly return to the United States when people around the world try to turn them into real estate, stocks, factories and tangible products before they are worth less. When this sudden flood of dollars pushes prices up, the United States will finally experience the hyperinflation that should have happened a long time ago but that was postponed because the other countries followed the game and were generous enough to accept taking those dollars away from the United States in exchange for its products and services.

When this scenario is carried out and everything collapses, the United States' trade deficit cannot be blamed. The real reason why this will happen is because the United States can finance the trade deficit with Fiat money created by the Federal Reserve. *If the money had never abandoned the gold standard and the banks could not manipulate it at will, the trade deficit would not exist.* It would be impossible. All the pessimistic scenarios of the future are rooted in the problem of Fiat money created out of nowhere by a group of private bankers.

Like the bankrupt consumer who stays afloat making only the minimum payments on his credit card, the US government has evaded bankruptcy by paying only the interest on his monstrous debt. The problem he faces is that soon, even that growing account could overflow and exceed what the government can afford to pay. The advantage is that while the debt remains in dollars, the government can print money to cover its insolvency. But if the dollar is dethroned and loses its status as a world reserve currency, the United States may end up in debt in some other currency, and bankruptcy would be inevitable. If the United States insinuates that it can no longer pay interest on its national debt, the planet's economy would collapse.

THE CONSPIRACY AGAINST THE DOLLAR

The United States is the only country in the world that can print all the paper that he want to trade with the whole world and preserve the value of the dollar for one reason only: it is the currency with which you can buy oil mainly. The problem facing Uncle Sam today is that things are changing.

Iran and several OPEC countries are stopping trading oil in dollars and are starting to use other currencies, such as the euro. If the oil no longer has to be traded in dollars, the central banks of the other countries will no longer have any interest in acquiring government bonds from the United States. British journalist John Pilger, writing in *The New Statesman* in February 2006, stated that the real reason for the aggressive US military threats against Iran was not based on Iran's nuclear ambitions, but on the effect of the world's fourth largest producer oil breaking the monopoly enjoyed by the dollar. The journalist also mentioned that Iraqi President Saddam Hussein had done the same before being destabilized and attacked. In an article in 2005, Mike Whitney warned what could happen if the "petrodollar" were abandoned:

"This is much more serious than a simple fall in the price of the dollar. If the biggest oil producers in the world pass from the dollar to the euro, the US economy would sink almost one day to another. If the oil were traded in euros, central banks around the world would feel forced to do the same and the United States would be required to pay its enormous dollar debt. That, of course, it would be the end for the American economy. If there is an easy solution, I have no idea what it could be. "

When Libya decided to trade oil in another currency, Gaddafi decided to accept euros as a means of exchange. This producing country began exporting oil and natural gas to Europe and accepting euros in return. We already know what happened to Gaddafi. Iraq had the same idea, and things took the same course. All those who have dared to challenge the petrodollar have ended up murdered and countries have been invaded under the pretext of "having massive destruction weapons" or "supporting terrorism." While it is true that some of the countries that have decided to invade the United States have been commanded by dictators, the real and only reason why

Uncle Sam intervenes is to protect their global empire and maintain the hegemony of the petrodollar.

The inconvenience that the United States has is that there are countries with which it cannot use the same tactics of intimidation, wars and coups. At present, China began to openly question the status of the dollar as a world reserve currency and wants to start trading globally with its own currency. That is one of the most serious problems that the United States has today. The trade war that we have today is due to this, and the fact that the Yuan is already accepted into the IMF as one of the reserve currencies (along with the yen, the euro, the pound sterling and, of course, the dollar, who tops the list) is a matter of concern for the United States. These currencies are the only ones with which the International Monetary Fund conducts its operations. In these currencies the world reserves are deposited. Having entered this select club, the currency of China now serves to rescue countries, give international loans and finance banks around the world. Yuan has become very important in international trade and in the stock market. This is the ranking of the power of the currencies that make up the IMF basket:

- The US dollar commands the list, with more than 40% of the portfolio.
- The euro comes next, with a little more than 30%.
- The Yuan is in third place, with approximately 10%.
- The Japanese yen is in fourth place with more than 8%.
- Finally, the pound sterling is in fifth place with 8%.

(Data of 2016)

How powerful is the dollar really versus the Yuan? That is the question. Since 2014, Forbes magazine made the following prediction:

1. The companies were negotiating more and more with the Chinese directly using the Yuan, due to the speed of profits that this generated.
2. 60% of companies showed that the Chinese Yuan has many advantages, such as not having the risk of changing to dollars first, and then to Yuan.
3. And finally, the Yuan has been acquiring a lot of power in recent years. China unseated the United States as the biggest trading country in the world in 2013.

The path that separates one currency from the other is becoming smaller every time. This is a developing issue, and we have to wait for the events to unfold in the coming years. The truth is that the commercial war today causes much concern and generates high volatility in the markets. The future of the dollar is uncertain.

BUILDING THE GLOBAL EMPIRE WITH DEBT

John Perkins was what he called an *Economic Gangster*, and his mission was to persuade Third World countries to accept large loans, of a much higher volume than necessary to develop their infrastructure. In addition, it was necessary to ensure that development projects were executed by US corporations, such as *Halliburton* and *Bechtel*. Once these countries were trapped in debt, the United States authorities, in alliance with the international aid agencies, were in a position to control those economies and canalize their oil and other natural resources according to the interests of the construction of a global empire. Like the Mafia, the Economic Gangsters grant favors, and when they return to claim their share, the claimed pay can take the following forms: captive votes in the United Nations, establishment of military bases or access to precious resources such as oil and the channel from Panama. In his revealing book, *Confessions of an economic hit man*, John Perkins mentions the following:

In the final analysis, the global empire depends, to a large extent, on the dollar continuing to function as the world's reference currency. And the right to print dollars is something unique to the United States. This is how we make loans to countries like Ecuador, in the full awareness that they will never be able to return them ever. In fact, we do not want them to honor that commitment, because it is the debt that assures our influence, our pound of flesh. Under normal conditions, over time we run the risk of emptying our own treasury; After all, no creditor can keep an unlimited number of defaulters. But ours are not normal circumstances. The United States prints bills that are not backed by any gold reserves. Or to be more exact, they are not backed by anything, except the general confidence worldwide in the capacity of our economy and in which we will know how to maintain the good order of the forces and resources of the empire created by us to sustain us.

The ability to print bills gives us immense power. It means, among other things, that we can continue to grant loans that will never be returned ... and that we ourselves can also accumulate a large amount of debt. At the beginning of 2003, the US national debt surpassed the shocking figure of $ 6 billion and threatened to reach $ 7 billion before the end of the same year: a debt of $ 24,000 per

US citizen, more or less. Many of the creditors are Asian countries, especially Japan and China, which buy US Treasury securities (mainly Treasury bills) from the proceeds of their sales on consumer goods - electronics, computers, automobiles, household appliances and clothing. Above all - to the United States and the world market.

As long as the world continues accepting the dollar as a reference currency, this excessive indebtedness will not be a great obstacle for the corporatocracy. But if the dollar were replaced by another currency, and if some of the creditor countries, Japan or China for example, decided to claim, the change in the situation would be drastic, and the United States would suddenly find itself in a rather precarious situation.

Now, the existence of such a currency is no longer hypothetical. Since January 1, 2002, the euro has existed on the international financial scene, with increasing strength and prestige every month. The euro offers an extraordinary opportunity to OPEC, if it were to retaliate for the invasion of Iraq or for any other reason decided to try the test of strength with the United States. If OPEC made the decision to replace the dollar with the euro as the monetary unit of the transactions, the empire would be shaken to the very foundations. If that happened, and if one or two of our big creditors demanded the return of what was owed, the impact would be enormous.

Currently, the public debt of the United States is estimated at more than $ 21 trillion. People have no idea what the word "trillion" means. If you started counting dollars at a rate of one per second, you would take:

- 12 days to count $ 1 million dollars.

- 32 years to count $ 1billion dollars
- 31,688 years to count $ 1 trillion dollars.

The global empire that has been built on the foundations of oil and debt is facing great difficulties. Their survival every day becomes more precarious. If history serves as a guide, its collapse is inevitable, as with all the great empires that have preceded us. It is exciting to be alive in this time of history. It's like witnessing the collapse of the Roman Empire, but with Wi-Fi.

SUMMARY

- The US agreement with the royal family of Saudi Arabia, the largest oil producer in OPEC included a commitment on the part of OPEC to sell the oil only in US dollars and, in exchange, Saudi Arabia would receive arms and the Saud's house would have the protection of the United States to stay in power.

- The US dollar, once the most valuable in the world for its exchange in gold, was now "backed" by oil. The countries were now obliged to acquire newly printed monopoly notes from the Federal Reserve to buy this essential resource.

- Why did petrodollars cause so much volatility and bubbles where they went? When banks obtain a lot of money in the form of deposits, their reserves increase and, subsequently, their loans increase. When banks lend, prices go up. When prices rise, banks lend more and more and more ... until the economy can no longer withstand more indebtedness.

- The reason why the United States is such a "rich" country today is because it is in the unique position of having its currency accepted as a world reserve currency. This advantage allows the United States to create money from out of nowhere to trade internationally, and the other countries have no choice but to accept it.

- As long as the dollar remains at the top as a trading currency, the United States may continue to spend more than it earns. But when the dollar collapses and countries and business partners do not accept it anymore, the free ride will end. When this happens, hundreds of billions of dollars that are now resting abroad will quickly return to the United States and finally experience the hyperinflation that should have happened a long time ago but that was postponed because the other countries followed the game and were generous enough for accepting to take those dollars away from the United States in exchange for their products and services.

- If the money had never abandoned the gold standard and the banks could not manipulate it at will, the trade deficit would not exist.

- Like the bankrupt consumer who keeps afloat making only the minimum payments on his credit card, the US government has avoided bankruptcy by paying only the interest of being a monstrous debt.

- If the dollar is dethroned and loses its status as a world reserve currency, the United States may end up in debt in some other currency, and bankruptcy would be inevitable.

- Iran and several OPEC countries are stopping trading oil in dollars and are starting to use other currencies, such as the euro. If the oil no longer has to be traded in dollars, the central banks of the other countries will no longer have any interest in acquiring government bonds from the United States.

- The real reason for the aggressive military threats by the United States against Iran was not based on Iran's nuclear ambitions, but on the effect of the world's fourth largest oil producer, breaking the monopoly enjoyed by the dollar. Iraqi President Saddam Hussein had done the same before being destabilized and attacked. The inconvenience that the United States has is that there are countries with which it cannot use the same tactics of intimidation, wars and coups, such as China.

- China began to openly question the status of the dollar as a global reserve currency and wants to start trading globally with its own currency.

SECOND PART

Become the Federal Reserve

"The only thing I can tell you is that the worst thing you can do is invest in cash"

–Warren Buffett

In this second part I will show you how you can print money legally, in the same way that the Federal Reserve does. Do not expect to understand the examples that we will discuss here immediately. Make sure you read them several times and meet with friends and expert advisors to discuss the topic and analyze them. This book should be read at least five times in order to understand it better.

In the first part we talk about the robbery that the banking system carries out every day throughout the world. In this second part, I will show you how you can turn the biggest thief of all (the bank) into your partner, and benefit from its massive printing of tickets.

Once you put into practice the methods taught in the second part, you will have your own money printing.

Chapter 1
Mc Billionaire

"I'm not in the hamburger business. My business is real estate. "

-Ray Kroc, founder of McDonald's

Q: Does the government care if you invest in real estate?

A: Actually, no.

Q: Does the government offer significant advantages if you invest in real estate?

A: Absolutely.

Q: But are there no risks when investing in real estate?

A: Maybe.

Q: Have the rich found ways to minimize these risks for their benefits?

A: Of course. And you will do it too.

Q: If it's that simple, why do not other investors follow this route and that's it?

A: Two reasons: For lack of knowledge and fear.

Q: Could you explain it better?

A: Most of those who claim to be "investors" are actually speculators. The speculators are not really investing, but they are betting. There's not much difference between betting at a casino in Las Vegas and betting that the properties will always go up in value. A genuine investor makes money no matter what direction the market takes.

Q: So the people who have the knowledge do it easily?

A: Unfortunately, no. The other reason that stops people is fear. Afraid of what? To fail. If a person believes that failure is bad, then he will never do anything. It is impossible to live without failing in something, unless you live with such caution that maybe you may not be living really. The real failure is not to try. Only those who push themselves to the limit, who are willing to face that pain, humiliation, or worse, will become champions. All others are condemned to watch the game from the bench.

Q: But I do not have university degrees or have any money. Can I still play this game, too?

A: You do not need a university degree or have a PhD at Harvard to play Monopoly in the real world. You just need to understand the game of the rich and put it into practice. Slowly. One asset at a time. Some of the richest people on the planet have not had formal studies or money when they started. Steve Jobs, Richard Branson, John D. Rockefeller, Andrew Carnegie and Bill Gates are some examples. Wealth is a state of mind, not a piece of paper hanging on a wall or numbers in a bank account.

Q: What do I have to know to start playing Monopoly in the real world?

A: I thought you would never ask me that.

REAL ESTATE = WEALTH

The winners of the modern economy will be those who recognize that money became a liability after 1971, and use them to acquire genuine assets that generate cash flow, adjust to inflation and have a minimum exposure to taxes. Which asset meets all these requirements? The real estate. It is important to remember that real estate is only active when it generates cash flow.

As long as central banks continue printing money, tangible assets such as gold and real estate will increase in value while paper money (backed by nothing) will continue to lose purchasing power. Those who park their money in savings accounts or mediocre investments will become poorer every day. As we saw in the first part, *the longer you hold a Fiat currency, the less value you will have.* The real value is in the assets, not in the money. Cash has long ceased to be king. The cash flow is the true king today. Let me show you an example.

Let's suppose you worked hard and saved $ 20,000. With that money, you can choose between these three options:

Option # 1: Invest $ 20,000 in paper assets or in a special account of the bank that pays 5% per year.

After 7 years, those $ 20,000 will have turned into $ 28,142 (without counting the taxes), assuming that the market remained constant.

Option # 2: Invest $ 20,000 from your own pocket and borrow $ 180,000 from the bank to acquire a rental property worth $ 200,000. For the purposes of this example, let's assume that income from income is offset by operating expenses and the mortgage, and property is appreciated 5% annually.

After 7 years, the property will be worth $ 281,000 and your profit will be $ 101,420 ($ 281,000 less what is owed to the bank for the loan).

Option # 3: Invest $ 20,000 from your own pocket and borrow $ 180,000 from the bank to acquire a rental property worth $ 200,000. Instead of letting the profit grow to a compound interest, you borrow the appreciation every 2 years and invest it in a new property at 10%.

After 7 years, assuming that the market remained stable, your four properties will be worth $ 2,022,218 and your initial investment of $ 20,000 will now have become $ 273,198.

This would show the summary of the three options:

Options	Net Worth after 7 years	Average Annual Return
Option #1	$28,142	5.8%
Option #2	$101,420	58.2%
Option #3	$273,198	180.9%

These examples are for educational purposes only and do not take some important variables, such as taxes. It should also be clear that while long-term real estate markets tend to rise, at some point they will suffer some decline and lose a percentage of their value. The booms do not last forever, and at some point the crack will come. This example only focuses on capital gains, that is, it does not take into account cash flow or tax benefits. Show how option 1 and 2 are clear examples of "parking money". Option 3 is the option chosen by those who play Monopoly in the real world. This is its formula:

1. Invest in an asset.
2. Leverage me to invest.
3. Recover my money.
4. Maintain control of the asset.
5. Move my money to a new asset.
6. Recover my money.
7. Repeat the process.

This formula is what is known as the speed of money. And that is really what this second part is about: learning to speed up your money and that of others to acquire the greatest amount of assets in the shortest possible time.

TURN THE BANK IN YOUR PARTNER

In the first part we talked a lot about banks and elite bankers. The fraud they do affects our lives and causes them to enslave millions of people around the world every day with debt. However, the bank is the most important player in the game, and unless you learn to associate and work with it, you will be another victim of its web. The bank will make you either poorer or richer. It all depends on what you use it for. If you use it to acquire liabilities, you will become poorer every day. If you use it to acquire assets, its act of prestidigitation will help you get rich. Banks are printing money out of nothing, and you, why do not you do the same? Borrowing money from the bank and having someone else pay your debt while you have a profit left is as if you were the one printing the money. Let's see how you can turn the bank into your best partner:

	You	Bank
Money	20%	80%
Property	100%	0%
Appreciation	100%	0%
Deductions	100%	0%

The bank is the best partner that exists! You only have to pay the loan and your interest, and if you did a good job, your tenant will pay for you. Also, if the loan is at a fixed rate (as it should be), then every year you will be paying less money (because inflation will cause these mortgage payments to lose purchasing power each time). And that's not to mention that the interest on the loan is deductible. People believe that to invest in real estate they need a lot of money, however, the previous table shows us that this is false. The bank will finance you most of your investment in real estate, and allows you to stay with the appreciation and deductions of the property, even if you only put 20%. But if you want to start a business, buy shares or cryptocurrencies, the safest thing is that the bank does not lend you anything. In other words:

- If you are going to buy a property of $ 100,000, the common thing is that you only need $ 20,000 from your own pocket.
- If you are going to buy $ 100,000 worth of shares, the common thing is that you need to have that full amount from your own pocket.

Therefore, in most cases, *real estate is the investment that requires less money.* Unlike other investments, banks will be willing to finance almost the entire investment. The amount they lend you, the frequency with which they do it and the interest rate they give you depend on you as an entrepreneur or investor: your credit scoring, your history, or whether you are going to invest as an individual or through a corporation. We will address these issues later.

How is it that an investment in real estate, with a valuation of 6% per year, is by far a better investment than actions that increase 10% annually? A word:

leverage.

When you leverage an investment, you reap the benefits of the total appreciation of the asset, regardless of whether you only put a small part of your money in the operation.

Let's first see what an investment in real estate would be like only taking into account the appreciation in a period of 30 years:

Property value:	$200,000
Initial investment:	$40,000 (20%)
Leverage:	$160,000 (80%)
Average valuation of 6% during 30 years, for a total of:	$1,083,678
ROI (Profit / investment) X100:	2709.195% or **90% per year**

Our ROI would be 90% per year. How incredible is that? And that does not even include the cash flow generated by the property or the tax exemptions. Also, remember that we take what the properties average, so that appreciation could be higher in many cases, as lower in some, depending on the local market.

Let's compare with the shares:

Value of shares:	$40,000
Initial investment:	$40,000
Leverage:	$0
Average valuation of 10% for 30 years, for a total of:	$634,524
ROI (Profit / Investment) X100:	1586.31% or **52.8% per year**

This is only based on appreciation. All the tax advantages that real estate has with respect to paper assets are not taken into account.

Now let's look at another example, taking into account the tax benefits and the cash flow.

How is it possible that an investment in real estate, with an annual return of 7%, is far better than an investment in paper assets with a 10% return?

Two words: Leverage and taxes.

Type of investment	Real estate	Shares
Investment	$ 100,000	$ 100,000
Leverage	$ 400,000	$ 0
Total invested	$ 500,000	$ 100,000
Earnings before taxes	$ 7,000	$ 10,000
ROI before taxes	**7%**	**10%**
Depreciation	$ 27,000	N/A
Passive loss	$ 20,000	N/A
Potential return (assuming 30% tax level)	$ 6,000	N/A
Profit after taxes	$ 13,000	$ 8,000
ROI after taxes	**13%**	**8%**

This is the analysis of the previous example:

✓ The gain of the shares is taxed at a rate of 20% for capital gains (it changes a little depending on the country), so the profit of $ 10,000 after taxes ends up being $ 8,000.

✓ The profitability is made to the money invested from one's own pocket. The profitability of the bank's money is not taken out, since what is sought is to see how your money has been paid.

✓ The depreciation per year is $ 27,000 dollars. It includes the structure of the building and its contents. In a chapter later we will explain the depreciation.

✓ The $ 7,000 is tax free after depreciation, and we also end up with a "passive loss" of $ 20,000, which can be used against other income. In this case, those $ 20,000 creditors make a potential return of $ 6,000, assuming that the income that is going to be offset is at a tax level of 30%. We will explain all this later. For the moment, the important thing is to see why investment in real estate is a unique investment.

NOTE: The percentages and figures used are hypothetical and vary depending on each country. We must also keep in mind that the tax law changes constantly so that the validity of this example can be altered. This information should not be used as a basis for making any financial decision. Taxes are a very complex issue and vary depending on the particular situation of each individual. The help of an expert in the subject is mandatory.

WHY INVEST IN REAL ESTATE?

These are some of the best reasons why you should invest in real estate:

- Cash Flow.
- Control
- Coverage against inflation.
- Leverage.
- Depreciation.
- Amortization.
- Refinance.
- Equivalent exchange (1031).
- Appreciation.

Let's begin by briefly analyzing them separately.

CASH FLOW

Every month, whether you work or not, you receive a passive income that has minimal exposure to taxes. If the real estate property is in an area where there are nearby jobs and where the supply is less than the demand, the occupation will be high and constant, assuring you a cash flow every month. In the end, the cash flow is what determines whether a property is an asset or a liability or whether it is a good, mediocre or bad investment.

These are the income that a professional real estate investor obtains:

1. Rent income: This is the profit you have left after paying all your expenses.
2. Income from capital gains (surplus value): If your rental income increases or you receive a valuation of your property, you as an investor can refinance and request a loan for the value of the goodwill as *tax-free* cash, and your tenant will pay this new loans. In other words, it is extra money free of taxes.
3. Revenue for amortization: The tenant will be responsible for paying the mortgage debt with their respective interests.
4. Income due to depreciation: It is considered a "Phantom Income". Although it appears as an expense, it is actually an income that comes from the tax legislation.

They can be better appreciated in the financial statement that appears below:

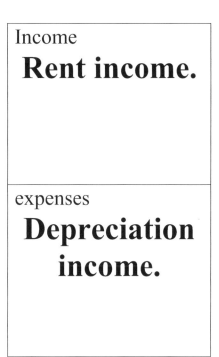

Income	
Rent income.	
expenses	
Depreciation income.	

Balance sheet

Assets	Liabilities
Income from capital gains (surplus value).	**Amortization (open debt).**

We will cover this income as we move forward.

CONTROL

If I buy Amazon stock, I doubt very much that Jeff Bezos answers my calls and considers my opinions on the management that should be given to the company. I totally depend on the people in charge of Amazon doing a good job. If they end up being incompetent, my actions end up being worth zero.

Real estate, with a good real estate administration and a good team of tax experts, leaves very few things at random and it is almost certain that the checks will arrive automatically. You can make decisions, sell when you want, low or raise rents, carefully select your tenants, hire or fire employees of the property and have real control over your property.

COVERAGE AGAINST INFLATION

If a "safe" investment pays you 2% or 3% per year, you are not really making money. In fact, you could be losing money. The reason is the following: inflation.

The middle class and the poor have to work harder and harder because wages, while rising, do not adjust to inflation. After many people earn their money with so much effort, they put it into the bank or any investment that pays 2% or 3%. The problem is that inflation exceeds these returns, evaporating any existing gains. If you have your money in a savings account that pays you 3% per year and inflation is 4% per year, you are getting poorer because the cost of goods and services is increasing in value faster than your money.

The beauty of real estate is that they increase along with inflation, or sometimes much more. That does not include cash flow, refinancing, depreciation and mortgage deductible interest. Inflation favors investors in real estate, while people with fixed income or savers discreetly stripped of their wealth.

LEVERAGE

How long would it take you to save a million dollars? How long would it take you to borrow a million dollars? Who is more financially intelligent? Someone who works physically all his life trying to save a million dollars? Or someone who knows how to borrow a million dollars and make a profit after covering all expenses?

It is very hard for the poor and the middle class to become rich because they try to use their own money to achieve it ... money they worked hard for and for which they have already paid up to 50% in taxes. If you want to be financially free, you need to learn how to use debt to get rich. Also, as we saw earlier, there is no difference between debt and money today. The most ironic of all is that the middle class and the poor think that using debt to acquire assets is risky, but they busily go out and use the debt to buy liabilities.

The advantage of real estate is that the bank is willing to finance up to 95% of the property on many occasions. As we saw in the previous examples, the leveraged investments are the ones that yield the highest yields. A person does not become a genuine investor until the moment he invests using leverage, that is, debt. Only lazy investors invest using their own money.

DEPRECIATION

Governments offer refuges and tax incentives to real estate for rent because they "lose value", although it is not common for them to do so. In fact, the reason why the government implements these fiscal policies and offers incentives for depreciation is because real estate investors provide housing ... and an important area in the economy is to provide housing. Something that should be clear is the following: depreciation can be applied even when the property is increasing in value. Later we will devote an entire chapter to talking about the best deduction of all: depreciation.

AMORTIZATION

When the poor and the middle class acquire debts, they run the risk and must pay these debts. However, when the rich acquire debts and use them to invest, they assume the risk but pay them. That is, they make sure that someone else will pay the debt with their respective interests. In real estate, you run the risk when you ask for a mortgage and, in return, your tenant pays it. The bank will lend you to acquire the property and your tenant will pay the bank. Never acquire a debt unless you know that someone else will pay it for you, that is, unless it is amortized.

REFINANCE

An amateur investor perceives an appreciation in his property and sells it, causing a tax event and exposing himself to high taxes. In addition, when selling the asset, it loses the cash flow it generates.

A sophisticated investor, on the other hand, perceives an appreciation in his property and instead of selling it he refinances it, obtaining money free of taxes, conserving the asset and its cash flow and making sure that the new debt continues to be paid by the tenant. We will devote an entire chapter to this, since refinancing plays a key role in the formula we discussed at the beginning of this chapter: *the speed of money.*

EQUIVALENT EXCHANGE (1031)

In the United States it is called *Exchange* 1031; in some countries it has the name of *equivalent exchange*. Its function is almost the same in all countries: you can sell real estate and defer your taxes for capital gains as long as you reinvest all the money in another property and meet certain requirements. If you bought and sold shares, you would have to pay taxes for the profits you made. But if you buy and sell real estate, you can defer your taxes indefinitely, reinvesting the capital and acquiring more properties. We will explain the procedure of this mechanism later.

APPRECIATION

While all currencies lose their value every day due to inflation, real estate is one of the main assets that tend to increase in value thanks to inflation. Instead of saving currencies that are worth less every day, when you buy real estate you will be exchanging a liability (currency) for an asset (real estate) that increases with inflation.

Although you must be careful. The problem of appreciation is that, in general, it only works in markets that are rising. If the market goes down (which always happens), playing "buy cheap and sell expensive" does not work. You should always invest in cash flow, because, in addition, the tax laws favor the investor in cash flow, not the investor in capital gains. Remember the golden rule of investments: your profit is when you buy, not when you sell.

The appreciation goes to the end because it is the last reason why you should invest. You should not even have it. Acquire real estate and wait for its value to increase is to bet, not invest. Investing looking for an appreciation can end up being tragic if a *crack* occurs in the real estate market, which happens regularly. Later I will show you how you can get a real appreciation and how you can take advantage of it, instead of waiting for certain conditions in the market that do not depend on you.

REAL ESTATE ARE LIABILITIES

Something that should be clear is that *real estate alone is liabilities; it is the derivatives of real estate that are considered assets.* Some derivatives are these:

Property Tax: Real estate can never be fully owned. If you think I am wrong, then stop paying your property taxes and you will meet the real owner of the land. One of the derivatives of a property is the property tax that you must pay to the government periodically. This tax is an asset of the government but a liability of yours. Remember that for every liability you have, you are the asset of someone else.

Mortgage: When a bank tells you that your house is an asset, it is not telling you lies. It's just that he's not telling you the whole truth. Your house is an asset of the bank, but a liability of yours. The mortgage is a derivative of real estate, and they generate money to the bank on a monthly basis.

Lease contract: A real estate investor does not primarily seek to own a property for the simple fact of having it, but seeks to find a tenant as soon as possible to sign a lease and start paying monthly rent. *The important thing is the cash flow, not the property itself.*

Banks do not really want real estate, but mortgages on real estate. Banks know that a property in itself is a liability and that is why they are auctioned off. Do you think that if the real estate alone were active, the banks would auction it off? Of course not. If there is no one who pays the mortgage or a tenant who pays the rent, the real estate is considered passive. At best, they can be considered "bets" and wait for their value to increase in the long term to sell more expensive and make a profit. Of course, until this does not happen, the bettor must classify your property as what it is: a liability.

Let's begin to delve into the subtitle of this book: *how to use debt and taxes to get rich.*

SUMMARY

- You do not need a university degree or a doctorate at Harvard to play Monopoly in the real world.

- The winners of the modern economy will be those who recognize that money became a liability after 1971, and use it to acquire genuine assets that generate cash flow, adjust to inflation and have a minimum exposure to taxes. Which asset meets all these requirements? The real estate.

- Real estate is only assets when it generates cash flow.

- The real value is in the assets, not in the money. Cash has long ceased to be king. The *cash flow* is the true king today.

- Although in the long term real estate markets tend to rise, at some point they will suffer some decline and lose a percentage of their value. The booms do not last forever, and at some point the *crack* will come.

- The bank is the most important player in the game, and unless you learn to associate and work with it, you will be another victim of its web.

- Banks are printing money out of nothing, and you, why do not you do the same? Borrowing money from the bank and having someone else pay your debt while you have a profit left is as if you were the one printing the money. Real estate can be your money printing shop!

- The real estate is the investment that less own money demand. Unlike other investments, banks will be willing to finance almost the entire investment. The amount they lend you, the frequency with which they do it and the interest rate they give you depend on you as an entrepreneur or investor.

- When you leverage an investment, you reap the benefits of the total appreciation of the asset, regardless of whether you only put a small part of your money in the operation.
- Why invest in real estate? 1) Cash flow, 2) Control, 3) Coverage against inflation, 4) Leverage, 5) Depreciation, 6) Amortization, 7) Refinancing, 8) Equivalent exchange (1031), 9) Appreciation.
- Real estate alone is liabilities; it is the derivatives of real estate that are considered assets.
- The important thing is the cash flow, not the property itself.

Chapter 2

The rich do not pay taxes ... legally

"I do not pay taxes."

–Donald Trump

Q: Who designs the laws?

A: The politicians.

Q: Who sponsors the politicians' campaign?

A: The rich.

Q: So, who *really* designs the laws?

A: The rich

In a 2007 article titled "*Who governs the United States?*" Professor James Petras observed:

"Within the dominant financial class, the political leaders come from the banks of private and public share capital, that is, Wall Street. They organize and finance the two major parties and their electoral campaigns. They press, negotiate and draft the most complete and favorable legislation on global strategies (liberalization and deregulation) and sectorial policies. They press the government to "rescue" unviable and bankrupt speculative firms,

to balance the budget by reducing social expenditures instead of increasing taxes on extraordinary speculative profits. These private equity banks are involved in all sectors of the economy and in all regions of the global economy. "

Was the tax law written for the rich?

Have you ever wondered where a large percentage of your money goes each month when you receive your paycheck? Is it mostly intended to cover social programs or something like that? Usually not. I will tell you where your taxes are going to stop: to the entrepreneurs and investors who act as the government wants.

The government drafts tax laws to incentivize certain activities that benefit the economy. These activities are carried out by entrepreneurs and investors. This means that if the government wants to encourage the creation of low-cost housing, they will provide a fiscal stimulus to motivate developers and investors to create real estate of these characteristics. If the government needs to create stable jobs for the middle class, the government will grant tax incentives to employers for hiring workers. You may ask yourself: "But the government still has to pay its bills. Who is taxed then? "I think you already know the answer: to the middle class. The middle class is responsible for subsidizing entrepreneurs and investors who behave like the government and the economy want to receive all the tax benefits.

Why does the government act like that? Simple: if you want to encourage investment in low-cost housing for low-income employees, you should give large tax deductions to real estate investors. If you want to encourage domestic oil production, you must give fiscal incentives to those who invest in the extraction of oil. If you want to create more jobs, you must award fiscally to employers who hire workers. Robert Kiyosaki explains this in the following way:

"I do not pay taxes because I create jobs. When I create a job, I create a taxpayer, and that's what the government needs ... taxpayers who pay taxes, invest in a pension fund and contribute to social security. "

Do not misunderstand what this book teaches: we are not talking about fiscal loopholes that are "unintended" consequences of enacted laws. It is not about evading taxes. Evading taxes is illegal. It is about the "intentional" consequences foreseen by the legislators. If you think that the rich evade taxes and cheat the middle and lower classes, none of this is for you. While there are some corrupt businessmen and politicians who do this, here we are talking about benefits that are in the tax law of almost all countries, which take advantage of entrepreneurs and investors that help the growth of a country's economy.

The rich pay little or no taxes because they improve the economy of a country. That's the truth. The following table explains it better:

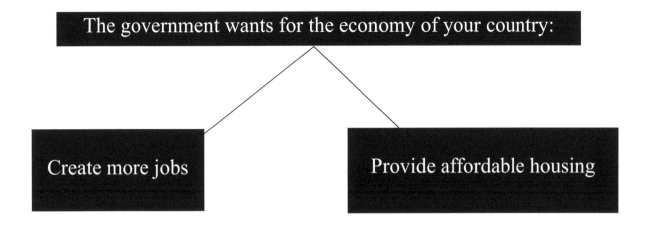

The government wants for the economy of your country:

Create more jobs

Provide affordable housing

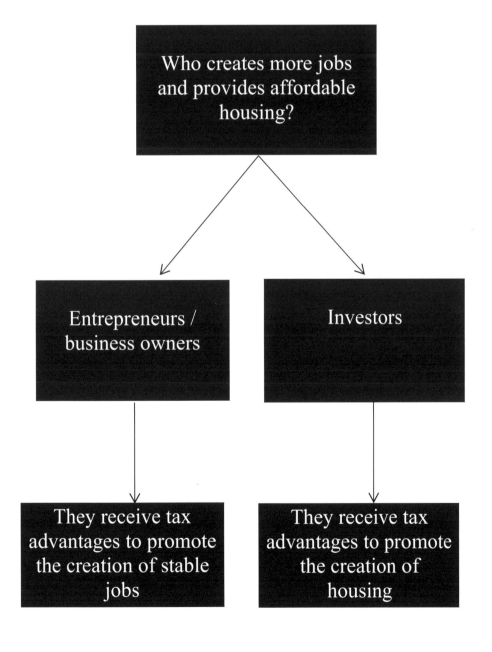

Who creates more jobs and provides affordable housing?

Entrepreneurs / business owners

Investors

They receive tax advantages to promote the creation of stable jobs

They receive tax advantages to promote the creation of housing

IT IS BAD TO PAY TAXES

The average taxpayer in a developed country spends up to 35% of his life working to pay taxes. More than two hours a day of each day of their work serve to feed the government. And he works almost four months every year to pay taxes. In total, this reaches more than 13 years of his working life and 20 years of his life. 20 years! That's the same as having been locked up in prison. Without a doubt it is a very strong sentence. And all for what? To promote social programs? Improve society? Promote infrastructure works? In most of the cases, no. As we saw in a previous chapter, the income tax was born to pay interest on the public debt. This means that most of these taxes are not going to anything productive. The only thing this money does is pay interest on the public debt. Even if you live in a country where the employer pays taxes on employment, think about how much money the average taxpayer would earn if he did not have to pay those taxes.

Paying taxes is not a patriotic act; It is an act of slavery. Most of the revolutions of the countries had as their main motivation the unjust and excessive taxes. The tax on tea in the United States is an example. It is very bad not to reduce your taxes. Not taking advantage of the advantages that exist in the law to help you means that you are robbing your family and your future.

HOW THE TAXES AFFECT YOUR INVESTMENTS

A sophisticated investor always analyzes the tax issue before investing. Next, you will find out why:

Investment: $ 10,000.

Year	Return of 10% and taxes of 40%	Return of 10% and without paying taxes
1	$10,616.77	$11,047.13
10	$18,193.96	$27,070.13
20	$33,102.04	$93,280.73
30	**$60,225.75**	**$198,373.99**

Taxes can make you very poor if you do not have a tax strategy! The second part of this book is precisely about that: create a fiscal strategy that is effective by accumulating a broad portfolio of real estate that generates cash flow.

You may wonder what kind of investment can pay 0% tax. The answer is: real estate. Investment in real estate should be analyzed after taxes. It is after taxes when real profits are made. Is that how it works:

Property	$ 1 million
Initial payment	$100,000
Loan	$900,000

Performance of the investment **before** taxes.

Income	$148,257
Operational expenses	$67,497
Net Operating Income	$80,760

Mortgage	$68,268
Cash flow before taxes	**$12,492**
ROI before taxes	**12.492%**

Performance of the investment **after** taxes.

Total depreciation	$25,994
Tax loss	$13,502
Potential return at a 35% tax rate	$4,726
Cash flow after taxes	**$17,218**
ROI after taxes	**17.22%**

That is an excellent return. And remember that it is increasing as inflation increases. The next chapter will explain carefully the depreciation and the fiscal or "passive" loss. For now I just want you to change your perspective on taxes and how they work.

DEDUCTIONS FOR EVERY CLASS

This is the difference between the deductions that exist between the rich and everyone else:

DEDUCTIONS	
Middle class / Low class	**Rich**
Mortgage interests	Supply for business
Property taxes	Equipment for business
Donations to foundations	Advertising or business marketing expenses
Personal exemptions	Home office expenses derived from business
	Use of the vehicle for business
	Dinners and meals in restaurants (as long as business is discussed)
	Travel and entertainment where it is shown to be related to the business
	Mortgage interests
	Property taxes
	Donations to foundations
	Personal exemptions

You are right in thinking that the tax law is not fair. It does not pretend to be fair. It intends to encourage certain activities. The most promoted activities are business and investments.

DO NOT BE LIKE THE AVERAGE TAXPAYER

The taxes are incredibly unfair to the average taxpayer. What characteristics does the average taxpayer have? The average taxpayer has a job, a family to maintain, a mortgage or rent and a pension plan. The average taxpayer has little or no financial education. As long as people live the life of the average taxpayer, there is nothing that can be done. The secret is to stop being average.

These are the differences between the average taxpayer and the rich taxpayer:

AVERAGE TAXPAYER	RICH TAXPAYER
He has a job	He creates jobs
He believes that his house is an asset	He invests in real estate that generates cash flow
He has a mortgage for his own home	He has many mortgages but for investment properties
He has a mediocre counter	He has a team of expert advisors in business and real estate issues
He invests using his money	He invests using someone else's money
He invests what he has left *after* paying taxes	He invests through a business with money *prior* to paying taxes
He focuses on his income	He focuses on his assets

You may think that you have no control over your taxes. Everyone has to pay high taxes, right? False! There are a lot of people who pay very little or no taxes all over the world legally. I want you to belong to this group and stop giving your money to a corrupt government that has no financial education and the only thing it knows how to do is spend public resources and get into debt.

SUMMARY

- Was the tax law written for the rich? Of course yes!
- Your taxes go to entrepreneurs and investors who act as the government wants.
- The middle class is responsible for subsidizing entrepreneurs and investors who behave like the government and the economy wants to receive all the tax benefits.
- We are not talking about fiscal loopholes that are "unintended" consequences of enacted laws. It is not about evading taxes. Evading taxes is illegal. It is about the "intentional" consequences foreseen by the legislators.
- The rich pay little or no taxes because they improve the economy of a country.
- Paying taxes is not a patriotic act; it is an act of slavery. Most of the revolutions of the countries had as their main motivation the unjust and excessive taxes.
- A sophisticated investor always analyzes the tax issue before investing.
- Investment in real estate should be analyzed after taxes. It is after taxes when real profits are made.

Chapter 3

Depreciation: *Ghost Income*

"In the new capitalism, those who know how to borrow money win, not those who save in a bank account. In the new capitalism, it makes much more sense to borrow money and pay it in the future with dollars that will be much cheaper then. If the US government does it, why do not we? The government is in debt; why not get into debt ourselves? "

–Robert Kiyosaki

Why did Donald Trump announce in his campaign for the presidency that he did not pay taxes? Why did he refuse to share his financial status like all the other candidates? Is it because it was tax fraud or tax evasion? No, of course not. No wonder Trump does not pay absolutely any taxes legally. Although I'm surprised he announced that publicly. One would think it is political suicide, since the great mass of society (which has no financial education at all) does not really understand why an entrepreneur the size of Trump said that. After this chapter, you will know why Donald Trump, the president of the United States, does not pay taxes legally. Let's start at the beginning.

GHOST INCOME

The ghost income is not visible, that is the problem. In no investment will it be visible nor will it be underlined by any side. It is not possible to see this income with the eyes. Amateur investors, some accountants and specialists sometimes overlook it and that is why they do not get the most out of their investments. It is not income earned (salary), neither capital gains nor liabilities. It is a ghost. It is a product of debt and taxes. The phantom cash flow is the real income of the rich. It is an invisible income that is derived from debt and taxes.

Let's analyze the following example of what would be a ghost income that the richest people in the world take advantage of

:

Value of the property	$300,000
Investment (20%)	$60,000
Leverage (80% mortgage)	$240,000

Rent	$28,000
Mortgage payments	$14,400
Expenses	$7,200
Cash Flow	**$6400**
ROI	**10.6%**

Interest on the debt (interest on mortgage payments)	$8,000
Passive loss	$1,600
Potential return (Ghost income)	$1,600
Total cash flow	**$8,000**
ROI	**13.3%**

The ghost cash flow in this case is $ 1,600. In this case, that passive loss is used against other passive income, so it is obtained in its entirety. Keep in mind that this varies a bit in each country and has some requirements, but it works well and is applicable worldwide.

This is the true income of the rich, and is the product of debt and taxes. Just as it impoverishes most people, it makes the rich richer. The interest on the debt of the previous example that caused the passive loss and therefore the potential return is not the only ghost income that exists. The appreciation, depreciation, amortization and more deductions from the tax code are examples of ghost income. Remember that this money is totally tax free.

In this chapter we will focus on debt and depreciation, but first, let's briefly define the best-known ghost income that exists:

- *Debt*: It is money exempt from taxes. Debt is a ghost income because you save money and time by renting tax-free money instead of working to earn it and paying taxes on it. In addition, by applying a refinance on your property, you are getting money free of taxes, that is, a ghost income that comes from the debt. In the next chapter we will thoroughly explain the refinancing.

- *Appreciation*: Appreciation is a ghost income that can be obtained in two main ways: refinancing or selling. The next two chapters will discuss both and how you can apply them to get a profit without triggering a tax event.

- *Amortization*: It refers to the reduction of your debt. Each time you pay a debt, the loan is amortized, that is, it is paid. Most people repay their debts with money for which they worked and for which they already paid heavy taxes. Professional real estate investors amortize their debts with the rent their tenant sends them. The advantage that real estate has is that you get into debt to acquire a property, but the tenant is the one who pays or *amortizes* the debt.

- *Depreciation*: Depreciation is a ghost income because you get a deduction for something that did not cost you any money. This deduction reduces or eliminates your taxes, putting more money in your pocket.

Never forget this formula:

More real estate = More ghost income

Why does it work like this? Because the more real estate you have, the more debt, amortization, appreciation and depreciation you will have (ghost income). Everything will grow exponentially. Instead of working in a job and making money linearly (because 1 hour of work equals X amount of money, and to increase X it is required to increase the number of hours worked first), use the tax-free debt to invest in real estate and increase your income exponentially little by little.

In this chapter we will explain two ghost incomes: debt and depreciation. In the following chapters we will study the assessment more thoroughly.

THE DEBT IS THE KEY

When the poor and the middle class save their money by parking it in the bank or under the mattress, the cash stops flowing and the economy stops. That's why the government charges these people high taxes. He punishes them fiscally for not keeping him in motion and for harming the system. If all the people of the world saved money nothing else, the world economy would suffer a collapse.

The key words today are: *do what the government wants*. The government desires and urgently needs debtors, since as we saw in the first part of this book, debt is the new money. Through taxes, the government gives incentives to people who get into debt and punish people who save. Money is created when someone asks for a loan, not when you and I save it. The global financial system needs debtors, not savers. Saving money in the post-1971 economy is financial suicide. If you park your money, its value decreases due to inflation. Any person in their right mind would ask: "Why am I going to save money if governments and banks are printing it in heaps? Why am I going to cling to a piece of paper that is worth less every day? "If the situation remains the same, saving money will be the most risky thing you can do and getting into debt to acquire assets will be the smartest thing you can do ... it all depends on your level of financial education.

The key to building long-term tax-free wealth in real estate is to keep buying more and more properties with debt. Without the leverage that debt provides, real estate is a mediocre and slow investment. The debt is what makes real estate work. The debt is what allows you to acquire properties that generate cash flow by putting little money on your part.

Despite what people believe, debt is very cheap compared to the income you earn from your salary. Debt is less expensive than estate. The estate is what you have left *after* paying taxes. This means that for an employee to invest $ 1,000, he has to work hard and earn approximately $ 1,666. In this case, using the estate to invest cost you 40%, or $ 666. On the other hand, you can invest the debt free of taxes. Even if the interest rate is between 5% and 8%, taking advantage of the debt is much cheaper because, otherwise, you would have to use the estate for which you already paid 40% of taxes (or even more). *It is cheaper, faster and smarter to learn how to borrow money to invest at a favorable interest rate than to work hard on a job for a paycheck and invest with what you have left after paying between 35-50% of taxes.*

Never forget it:

The debt decreases your taxes, while the savings increase them.

DEPRECIATION

The most important deduction of all is depreciation. All other deductions cost you money, except depreciation. Depreciation is like magic: you receive a deduction for something that did not cost you money. Depreciation is like creating money from out of nowhere. Depreciation is the key and every professional investor must examine it well before investing in a property.

When you buy an investment property that generates cash flow in the form of income, you can deduct a percentage each year that you own it. This deduction is known as depreciation. Not only do you receive deductions for depreciation in real estate. You can also receive deductions for depreciation by your business team. Many times you can even include your car, as long as its main use is business. You could even include a part of your house that you use as an office. The possibilities for business owners and investors are endless and the tax law is on their side.

This is how depreciation basically works in real estate:

Annual rental income	$ 12,000
Depreciation	$ 17,000
Passive loss	$ 5,000
Tax refund potential (assuming tax level of 40%)	$ 2,000

The $ 12,000 of income is tax free thanks to the $ 17,000 of depreciation. In addition, there is a passive loss that can be used against other income. It must be clarified that in this example, passive loss is used to offset an earned income (salary), but in some countries it is passive loss can only be used against other passive income.

These are the main formulas we will use for this chapter.

- (Total value of the asset - Total value of the land) / Depreciable years = Annual depreciation of the property
- (Total value of contents) / Depreciable years = Annual depreciation of contents
- Annual Total Depreciation = Annual property depreciation + Annual depreciation of the contents

In a gift section are all the formulas that a professional real estate investor needs. In *How to play Monopoly in the real world* we already work with some of them, so if you have doubts about its operation and application, I recommend that you review the examples that this book brings.

In the United States, percentages work like this:

- Depreciation of residential properties: 3.6% for 27.5 years.
- Depreciation of commercial properties: 2.56% for 39 years.

These percentages may vary depending on the country, but the concept is the same. For purposes of this book, we will work the examples with the percentages of the United States, but you should know that regardless of the country where you live, as long as it is a capitalist country, the essence of all this is the same. In fact, in some countries, depreciation is known as *capital cost allocation*. It's a different name for the same thing. Apply the same accounting principles; do not be fooled by the language.

One thing you should have clear is that not only do you receive a deduction for the money you put in the property, but you can also deduct the money that the bank puts in your property. This means that you receive depreciation for the total cost of the property, even if you paid it with borrowed money. What's more, your property can be valued and even then you receive a deduction for depreciation.

That is magic. And that is the reason why the rich get richer: because they know how to use debt and taxes to enrich themselves. Let's analyze the following example.

For this example, we will only depreciate the property. We will not take into account the contents, but remember that with good tax advice and segregation of costs, the contents can be depreciated at a higher rate than real estate, sometimes up to 20%. That is a tremendous impact on your cash flow. Later I will show you how.

For this example, the depreciable years of the property are 27.5 years, which are those that apply to residential properties in the United States, but you should bear in mind that in each country this percentage changes.

Property value	$20,000,000
Land value	$5,000,000
Total depreciable value	$15,000,000
Annual depreciation	$540,000

This depreciation applies to the cash flow of the property. The $ 540,000 per year can be used against income from property.

Total incomes	$3,000,000
Operational expenses	$1,800,000
Net operating income	$1,200,000
Mortgage / annual debt	$900,000
Cash Flow	$300,000
Depreciation	$540,000
Passive loss	$240,000

Depreciation allows the $ 300,000 cash flow to be totally tax-free. In addition, there is an extra depreciation that is called "passive loss" of $ 240,000, which can be used against other income. This passive loss is allowed to be done even if $ 300,000 is earned and the property is being valued. This means that the total cash flow is $ 300,000 plus the potential tax refund of the passive loss of $ 240,000.

Thanks taxes!

COST SEGREGATION

Each investor must separate the cost of improvements to the land, the contents of the property and the land. What is inside the property must be separated from the physical structure on your tax return. This separation process is called *cost segregation or real estate valuation.*

Gardens, exterior improvements, fencing, parking, floor covering, curtains, cabinets, lighting, floors, window coverings, exterior lighting, fences, covered parking spaces and more objects, can depreciate faster than property, putting more money in your pocket faster. Everything except the earth is subject to depreciation.

The key is to correctly document the values of all the objects you depreciated through a cost segregation or a real estate valuation. Without that segregation, the tax collector can make all your tax savings for depreciation disappear.

How does cost segregation work? It determines the portion of the purchase price that you paid for the land, the property, the contents and the improvements to the land. While you receive a deduction for depreciation of 2.5-3.6% on the property, you will receive a deduction for depreciation of 15-20% or more for the content and 5-10% for land improvements.

When you perform a cost segregation, no matter how many years later, you can replenish all the depreciation you would have received from applying the cost segregation in the year of purchase. This is important to know in case you already have several properties and have not applied any of this in the past. Make sure to consult your tax advisor.

Next I will show you a complete example of how cost segregation works and how you should work your investments:

Cost of apartment ownership	$1,000,000
The value of the land	$200,000

Equal to the value of the building and content	$800,000
DEPRECIATION OF THE BUILDING	
Value of the building and content	$800,000
Minus building contents	$100,000
Equal to the value of the building	$700,000
Multiply the value of the building with a depreciation rate for residential properties	3.6%
Equal to the depreciable value of the building per year	**$25,200**
DEPRECIATION OF CONTENTS	
Contents of the building	$100,000
Multiply the value of the building's content by the depreciation rate	20%
Equal to the depreciable value of the content	**$20,000**

TOTAL DEPRECIATION OF THE BUILDING AND CONTENT	
Deduction for depreciation of the building	$25,200
Plus the deduction for content depreciation	$20,000
Equal to the total value of depreciation	**$45,200**

FISCAL IMPLICATIONS	
Cash flow of the property (income and other income after covering the mortgage and operating expenses)	$15,000
Minus the total deduction for depreciation	$45,200
Equal to a passive loss of	$30,200
The $ 15,000 in cash flow is totally tax-free.	

POTENTIAL TAX REFUND	
Amount of loss that can be used against other incomes.	$30,200
Multiplied by 40% (particular tax level assumed)	40%
Equal to a potential tax refund of	**$12,080**

What does this tell you? That the government will pay your investment in real estate.

In this case, that fiscal or passive loss was used against ordinary income, but sometimes it can only be made against another passive income. You must bear in mind that this varies a bit depending on the country but it is basically the same concept throughout the world.

That refund can be used to reinvest in another property, have an emergency fund, or to go on vacation.

You can benefit from depreciation even if your property is being valued. This tax refund for the passive loss you receive even if you are earning $ 15,000.

Thanks taxes!

With this level of leverage and with a cash flow free of taxes, investments at some point will begin to grow exponentially. Did you think Monopoly was just a game?

INVESTMENT PERFORMANCE	
Total value of the property	$1,000,000
Initial payment (20%)	$200,000
Bank loan (80%)	$800,000
Total profit (property income plus income from potential tax refunds)	$27,080
ROI (Profitability = Net Profit / Investment)	**0.135 o 13.5%**

OBSERVATIONS:

1. The profitability is done by analyzing the invested value of the own pocket, that is, in this case, $ 200,000. In this case, the money that the bank placed for the calculations is not taken into account since your interest is to analyze the performance of your money, not the bank's. Although, of course, you

benefit as much from your money as from the money that the bank placed in the operation.

2. The income of $ 15,000 is the income after having subtracted the operational expenses and interest on the debt, that is, it is the total cash flow that ends up in your pocket.

3. The profitability (ROI) is as follows:

$$ROI = (\$\ 15,000 + \$\ 12,080) / (\$\ 200,000)\ X100$$

$$ROI = 13.5\%$$

What does this mean? That in a little over 7 years you would recover all your money. This can be accelerated by applying a refinance to the property, something that we will explain in the next chapter.

4. In this example, the deductions that apply for the interest payment of the mortgage are not taken into account. This would make our cash flow and our ROI even higher. In future examples we will take into account the deductions for the payment of interest on the debt.

5. Our total cash flow is: Property cash flow ($ 15,000) + Potential return ($ 12,080) which would give a total of $ 27,080.

NOTE: The percentages and figures used are hypothetical and vary depending on each country. We must also keep in mind that the tax law changes constantly so that the validity of this example can be altered. This information should not be used as a basis for making any financial decision. Taxes are a very complex issue and vary depending on the particular situation of each individual. The help of an expert in the subject is mandatory. The fact that you understand the taxes and understand the tax law does not mean you can apply it alone. These examples are for educational purposes and are simply intended to serve as a guide so you know what to ask a specialist and what to look for in an investment.

Let's study the following example to make sure we understand how depreciation and cost segregation work:

Cost of commercial property	$900,000
Minus the value of the land	$100,000
Equal to the value of the building and contents	$800,000
DEPRECIATION OF THE BUILDING	
Value of the building and contents	$800,000
Minus building contents	$100,000
Equal to the value of the building	$700,000
Multiply the value of the building with a depreciation rate for commercial properties	2.5%
Equal to the depreciable value of the building per year	**$17,500**
DEPRECIATION OF CONTENTS	
Contents of the building	$100,000
Multiply the value of the building's content by the depreciation rate	20%
Equal to the depreciable value of the content	**$20,000**

TOTAL DEPRECIATION OF THE BUILDING AND CONTENT	
Deduction for depreciation of the building	$17,500
Plus the deduction for content depreciation	$20,000
Equal to the total value of depreciation	**$37,500**

FISCAL IMPLICATIONS

Cash flow of the property (income and other income after covering the mortgage and operating expenses)	$12,000
Minus the total deduction for depreciation	$37,500
Equal to a passive loss of	$25,500
The $ 12,000 in cash flow is totally tax-free.	

POTENTIAL TAX RETURN

Amount of loss that can be used against other income.	$25,500
Multiplied by 40% (particular tax level assumed)	40%
Equal to a potential tax refund of	**$10,200**

INVESTMENT PERFORMANCE	
Total value of the property	$900,000
Initial payment (20%)	$180,000

Bank loan (80%)	$720,000
Total profit (property income plus income from potential tax refunds)	$22,200
ROI (Profitability = Net Profit / Investment)	**0.123 o 12.33%**

OBSERVATIONS:

1. The profitability is made by analyzing the invested value of the own pocket, that is, in this case, $ 180,000. In this case, the money that the bank placed for the calculations is not taken into account since your interest is to analyze the performance of your money, not the bank's.

2. The income of $ 12,000 is the income after having subtracted the operational expenses and interest from the debt, that is, it is the total cash flow that ends up in your pocket.

3. The profitability (ROI) is as follows:

$$ROI = (\$12{,}000 + \$10{,}200) / (\$180{,}000) \times 100$$

$$ROI = 12.3\%$$

What does this mean? That in a little over 7 years you would recover all your money. This, again, can be accelerated by applying a refinance to the property.

NOTE: The percentages and figures used are hypothetical and vary depending on each country. We must also keep in mind that the tax law changes constantly so that the validity of this example can be altered. This information should not be used as a basis for making any financial decision. Taxes are a very complex issue and vary depending on the particular situation of each individual. The help of an expert in the subject is mandatory.

... MORE DEDUCTIONS

So far we have only taken into account depreciation and passive loss, but we have ignored the fact that the tax law offers a deduction for the payment of interest on the debt (mortgage).

If we consider these deductions to the previous examples, we would have returns (ROI) of up to 20%. Compare that with the 2% paid by the bank or the 4% that an average investment pays you. And that's not to mention that those investments are highly taxed with the highest tax rates. Let's see the following example.

Investment details:

Value of the property	$500,000
Investment (20%)	$100,000
Leverage (80%)	$400,000
Income per year	$56,000
Operational expenses	$20,000
Net Operating Income	$36,000

This would be the performance of our investment before including taxes, depreciation, passive loss and deductions for the payment of interest on the debt:

Annual mortgage	$29,000
Cash Flow	$7,000
ROI	**7%**

When we include all the tax advantages, our performance changes incredibly:

Annual mortgage after the deduction for interest payments	$17,000
Cash flow (annual NOI- Mortgage after deduction)	$19,000
Total depreciation (including content and structure)	$26,000
Passive loss	$7,000 ($26,000-$19,000)
Potential return at a tax level of 35%	$2,450
Total cash flow (cash flow + potential return)	$21,450
ROI	**21.45%**

After applying the deduction given for paying the interest on the debt, which in this case was $ 12,000 ($ 29,000 - $ 17,000), the Net Operating Income (NOI) ($ 36,000) is subtracted from the new mortgage ($ 17,000) to know the new cash flow. The resulting cash flow ($ 19,000) depreciation is subtracted ($ 26,000) and is totally tax-free. Then, there is a "passive loss" or "fiscal loss" ($ 7,000) that provides a potential return of money that can be used against other income. In this case, it is used against an income that is taxed at the rate of 35%, so the return would be $ 2,450. Keep in mind that in some countries passive loss can only be used against other passive income, so it could not be used against ordinary income that pays 35% in taxes. This variation must be taken into account since it changes in each country.

Finally, the final ROI ends up being the sum of the cash flow plus the tax refund ($ 19,000 + $ 2,450), divided by the invested capital ($ 100,000), and this result is multiplied by 100 to find the percentage, which in this case is of 21.45%. A return more than 3 times higher (7% to 21.45%) after including taxes and tax advantages.

THE TRUTH ABOUT TAXES AND REAL ESTATE

Real estate is such a good tax shelter that a serious real estate investor should never pay taxes for their cash flow or profits from a real estate sale. The principles of cash flow, leverage and depreciation apply to any property regardless of size and regardless of the country where it is located (provided it is a capitalist country).

As I tried to demonstrate you in this chapter, debt and taxes are fundamental for anyone who wants to be a professional real estate investor, since the tax benefits of long-term real estate investment can be equal to or even greater than the cash flow and increase in the value (appreciation) of your properties.

What we saw in this chapter was a magic trick known by the name of *depreciation*. One of the ways in which the rich create money out of nowhere is through real estate. You can have the government subsidize your business and your property, or pay for your vacations or improvements to your home, with the simple magic of depreciation. Amateur investors know only one way to make money from their investments: with appreciation. Legitimate investors do not think in terms of appreciation, but in terms of depreciation. Now you know why.

In short, taxes make the rich richer.

SUMMARY

- The ghost cash flow is the real income of the rich. It is an invisible income that is derived from debt and taxes.
- The appreciation, depreciation, amortization and more deductions from the tax code are examples of ghost income.
- Never forget this formula: *More real estate = More ghost income*
- When the poor and the middle class save their money by parking it in the bank or under the mattress, the cash stops flowing and the economy stops. That's why the government charges these people high taxes.
- If all the people of the world saved money nothing else, the world economy would suffer a collapse.
- The key words today are: *do what the government wants*. The government desires and urgently needs debtors, since as we saw in the first part of this book, debt is the new money.
- Through taxes, the government gives incentives to people who get into debt and punish people who save.
- The key to building long-term tax-free wealth in real estate is to keep buying more and more properties with debt. Without the leverage that debt provides, real estate is a mediocre and slow investment. The debt is what makes real estate work.
- The debt decreases your taxes, while the savings increase them.
- Depreciation is like magic: you receive a deduction for something that did not cost you money. Depreciation is like creating money from out of nowhere

- In some countries, passive loss can only be used against other passive income.

- In some countries, depreciation is known as *capital cost allocation.* It's a different name for the same thing. Apply the same accounting principles; do not be fooled by the language.

- One thing you should have clear is that not only do you receive a deduction for the money you put in the property, but you can also deduct the money that the bank puts in your property.

- Gardens, exterior improvements, fencing, parking, floor covering, curtains, cabinets, lighting, floors, window coverings, exterior lighting, fences, covered parking spaces and more objects, can depreciate faster than property, putting more money in your pocket faster. Everything except the land is subject to depreciation.

- Real estate is such a good tax shelter that a serious real estate investor should never pay taxes for their cash flow or profits from a real estate sale.

Chapter 4

Refinance: Tax free money

Monopoly Rule: Monopoly is a game of buying green houses and then exchanging them for red hotels. It is not a game of "buy cheap and sell expensive". It is a game of "cash flow".

One of the biggest benefits of real estate is that the loans do not pay taxes. Many amateur investors sell the property as soon as it rises in price because they believe it is the only way to recover their money. Instead of selling the property to make a profit and pay high taxes, you can request a loan from the bank through a refinance and you will not pay taxes for that capital. Instead of withdrawing your money and paying taxes, why not refinance the property? Refinancing gives you a tax-free credit and allows you to keep your assets! Remember: refinancing is a tax-free transaction in all capitalist countries. In no country will you be taxed if you get into debt, but on the contrary, they will give you deductions and benefits for getting into debt. You already know why this works like this: because debt is the new money, and the only way for the modern economy to grow and the system to keep working is for you and me to become indebted. If governments collected taxes from people for borrowing money, banks would close their doors and the system would collapse.

Do not worry if investing the cash flow of the property is not very high. With that you achieve an annual yield of 5-8% you can feel at ease. If you chose a good market to buy the property and manage it correctly, in a few years it will have been valued (either by external conditions or by an increase in the operations of the same) and you can recover your money faster with a refinance. After all, that's what this is about: getting your money back as quickly as possible, keeping the asset and getting an infinite ROI (return). This chapter will explain all this.

In a refinancing, the first thing you do is contact the lenders and get quotes. At the same time, property operations must be analyzed to determine what type of new loan the property can hold. The high payment of the mortgage should not be a problem because, as a result of the excellent administration, the cash flow is higher in the property than when it was acquired. Once quotes have been obtained, review the interest rates, closing costs and analyze how the new loan will affect the cash flow. Then, the last thing that is done is to choose the best loan according to the particular needs.

We will analyze two scenarios in the following pages: one in which refinancing can be a terrible idea, and another in which it is the most sophisticated and intelligent option that can be taken. Keep in mind that there is no single answer since each particular situation is different and requires an analysis of its own.

BE CAREFUL WHEN REFINANCING

Refinancing is a valid option if you are able to cover the new mortgage that your properties will have after refinancing. The problem is that many small properties will hardly continue producing cash flow after applying a refinance.

In small properties, the appreciation will generally be greater than the increase in rents. Small properties tend to appreciate at a higher rate than rents increase.

In large complexes, however, the appreciation will be related to the operations of the property. That is, the rents and the value of the property will increase at par, which is why there are more chances of success when refinancing in larger housing complexes (multifamily) than in individual (single family) dwellings.

Keep in mind that every business is different. Sometimes, individual properties can be refinanced, take out the allowed capital free of taxes and still to continue receiving positive cash flow from the property. That would be ideal. Each business must be considered separately. Everything varies depending on the interest rates of the new mortgage and how you manage the operations of the property.

Let's look at an example for the case in which you have a portfolio of individual homes and you want to refinance them all, but they would not support a refinancing, that is, they would stop giving you cash flow:

10 individual properties	For a total of $ 2 million
Each property	$200,000
Initial revenue	$ 1,000 per month for each unit
Revenue after 5 years	$ 1,170 per month for each unit

These would be the operations of the property before applying a refinance:

Income of revenues per monthly unit	$1,170
Operating expenses per monthly unit	$250
Mortgage payments per monthly unit	$867
Cash flow per monthly unit	$53
Cash flow for the 10 properties per year	**$6,360**

Each property was purchased for $ 200,000. Assuming 6% appreciation per year, each property, after 5 years, is worth $ 252,495.

At that point, you have $ 52,495 extra in each unit. The total would be $ 524,950 (for the 10 properties), from which 80% can be refinanced (sometimes more, sometimes less), that is, $ 41,996 per unit or $ 419,960 in total.

This new loan changes the mortgage payments. They go from being $ 867 per month per unit to $ 1,094. This would show the operations after applying a refinancing:

Income of revenue per unit	$1,170
Operational expenses per unit	$300
Mortgage payments per unit	$1,094
Cash flow per unit	-$224
Cash flow for the 10 properties per year	**-$26,880**

Per year, it would add $ 26,880 out of pocket! At that rate you will never be free financially. One solution would be to sell all of your properties and make an equivalent exchange for larger properties that can be refinanced and still produce positive cash flow. The beauty of equivalent exchange (1031 exchange in the United States) is that you can defer taxes on capital gains. The next chapter will explain this.

Remember that not all properties are the same. Sometimes, small properties can be refinanced and even give cash flow. Each business is different and must be evaluated separately.

INFINITE ROI = PRINT MONEY

In any investment, the goal is to have the highest return on investment (ROI) possible. Maximizing ROI is the key to any investment. However, in this chapter I will not teach you to maximize ROI, but to make it *infinite*. What does it mean to have an infinite ROI? That you are making money for nothing, in the same way that banks make money in exchange for nothing by printing money. An infinite ROI is the same as saying that you are printing money. If you have an asset that pays you $ 100 a month, but you do not have any *money of your own* invested in that asset, that means that your ROI, by definition, is infinite and that you are printing money.

Let's suppose you have $ 100,000 to invest. You have these 3 options:

Option 1: Invest $ 100,000 in a single property that generates an annual yield of 6%, not including taxes and deductions. After seven years, the property is now worth $ 120,000, but you decide not to get involved with the bank or ask for any credit or mortgage on the property.

Option 2: Invest $ 20,000 in five properties (for a total of $ 100,000) and borrow from the bank the remaining $ 80,000, where each one generates an annual return of 6% after making the mortgage payments and without including taxes and deductions. You decide to keep these investments in the long term and recover your money little by little at a rate of 6% per year. After seven years, you discover that each of your properties is now worth $ 120,000, but you prefer not to get this appreciation or selling or refinancing.

Option 3: Invest $ 20,000 in five properties (for a total of $ 100,000) and borrow from the bank the remaining $ 80,000, where each one generates an annual return of 6% after making mortgage payments and not including taxes and deductions. You decide to refinance each of the properties seven years later, when you discover that each property you bought for $ 100,000 is now worth $ 120,000. You recover your down payment on each property ($ 20,000 each, $ 100,000 in total), keep all the assets that continue generating cash flow and repeat the process.

Let's study how things look in the three options after a period of seven years (deductions and rent increase are not taken into account):

	Option 1	Option 2	Option 3
Own money initially invested	$100,000	$100,000	$100,000
Leverage	$0	$400,000	$400,000
Annual yield	6%	6%	**Infinite**
Number of properties	1	5	5
Value of the asset portfolio	$120,000	$600,000	$600,000

Let's analyze what happened:

1. Option 1 is the most mediocre option of all. While it is better to leave money in the bank, it is not the way a professional invests. An investor is considered sophisticated when he invests using someone else's money. Without debt, real estate is a mediocre investment.

2. Option 2 is a good option since debt is used to acquire a greater amount of assets in a shorter time. In this option, we converted $ 100,000 dollars into assets that generate cash flow of $ 500,000 and then $ 600,000 thanks to the appreciation suffered by the real estate. In addition, the money that the bank put in is tax-free money and the mortgage interest is deductible.

3. Option 3 requires a lot of financial education and is an aggressive strategy that is implemented around the world. It is the formula mentioned above known by the name of *the speed of money*. In this option, we converted $ 100,000 dollars into assets that generate cash flow of $ 500,000 and then $ 600,000 thanks to the appreciation suffered by the real estate. In addition, the money that the bank put in is tax-free money and

the mortgage interest is deductible. The difference with respect to option 2 is that after seven years, the total appreciation suffered by the real estate was used to request refinancing, obtain the return down payment, keep the asset, continue receiving money from each asset and repeat the process by acquiring new properties using the money obtained from refinancing ... all without paying any taxes.

Keep in mind that we do not take into account many factors, such as deductions, the increase in income in each option and the interest rate when refinancing in option three. This example, however, is applied worldwide by sophisticated investors, in all types of properties and in a way very similar to that shown in the example. The key to successful refinancing is to follow the following step:

1. Refinancing at an interest rate equal or lower than that acquired in the previous debt.
2. Make sure that the increase in the price of the property is accompanied by an increase in the rent of the same. If the price of property increased drastically but rents remained constant or rose very little, this is an indication that speculation is taking hold in the sector and people will start doing stupid things.
3. Manage the property correctly.
4. Reinvest again the money obtained through a refinancing in other properties.

Let's study the following example with larger numbers:

Price of the property	$ 20 million
Leverage (80%)	$ 16 million
Invested heritage (20%)	$ 4 million

	First year	Third year	Fifth year
Value of the property	$ 20 million	$ 25 million	$ 30 million
Debt	$ 16 million	$ 20 million	$ 24 million
Heritage	$ 4 million	$ 5 million	$ 6 million
NOI	$ 1 million	$ 1.4 million	$ 1.8 million
Annual mortgage	$800,000	$ 1 million	$1.2 million
Cash flow before taxes	$200,000	$400,000	$600,000
ROI	5%	*Infinite*	*Infinite*

COMMENTS:

1. The first year, the Net Operating Income was $ 1 million and the cash flow before taxes (that is, the annual NOI-Mortgage) was $ 200,000. The return on investment (ROI) was a modest 5% per annum (200,000 / 4 million X 100). To simplify this example, ghost income was not taken into account and simple numbers worked.

2. Note how the NOI increases in the third year, that is, the incomes increase. This increase in income causes the property value to increase due to this formula:

$$\text{Value of the property} = \frac{NOI}{Capitalization\ rate}$$

Do not worry about the capitalization rate. This information will be given by your real estate broker. If you have trouble understanding this formula and how it works, in *How to play Monopoly in the real world*, I explain it in detail. For the moment, what you should know is that an increase in the NOI causes an increase in the value of the property. For the third year, the value of the property was $ 25 million. The bank recognizes this increase in its value and grants us a loan for 80%, that is, for $ 20 million. This loan serves to settle the previous debt of $ 16 million and we have an additional gain of $ 4 million totally free of taxes. This money can be used to buy a new house, go to travel, go on vacation or reinvest in a new property and repeat the whole process. By refinancing the property in this way, I can obtain the valuation without selling the property and without incurring the high tax payment for the capital gains. The best part is that I keep controlling the asset, obtaining cash flow and, from then on, my ROI by definition is infinite. In this example, from the third year, I am already printing money legally, as do all the banks in the world.

3. For the fifth year we returned to the bank, we showed the increase of the ION, the bank made a valuation of the property for $ 30 million and gave us a loan for 80%, or $ 24 million. We pay off the previous loan of $ 20 million and again we get a $ 4 million profit tax free that can be used for anything. Some time ago we have an infinite ROI, but at this point, the property has ceased to be a simple property and has practically become a money printing company.

4. From the first day, the business was a winning business that produced cash flow. If the economy had collapsed and the value of the real estate had sunk, we would also have a

property that generates a return of 5% per year. It is important to remember this: the investment must make sense in a good and bad economy. At no time should you invest while waiting for the price of the asset to increase. The same thing that should be considered is that a large property is not very affected by market conditions. A property of $ 20 million like the previous example depends on its operations, that is, its NOI. The NOI in properties of these characteristics is what determines its value. On the other hand, in smaller properties, the value depends almost entirely on the sector where it is located.

KEYS FOR THE PREVIOUS EXAMPLE TO WORK

Possibly you think that the above is very good to be true, that it does not work that simple or that it does not apply to all countries. However, many investors apply the same strategy all over the world, every day at all times. While it is true that it is a very summary example that omits many details and is designed for educational purposes, it works very similar in the real world. If you want to belong to the few who make a deal of that style work, pay attention to these keys:

1. If it is a multi-family dwelling, the value will be determined by the NOI. That is, if you manage the property well, you add improvements and the rents increase, the value of the property increases. The bank recognizes this increase since the formula we used earlier explains this. If, on the other hand, it is a single-family home, the increase in its value will depend mostly on the market, that is, on factors that are foreign to you. However, if you bought in an area of high occupation where

there are stable jobs and people are beginning to move there, then the chances of the property increasing in value are high.

2. The interest rate given by the bank is key for this to work. If you have a good credit history, invest through a business and have consultants to help you, the bank may provide you with a rate below the market level. The impact of the new debt on cash flow should be analyzed.

3. To ensure that the property is valued and you do not have to depend on the market or external conditions, you must add improvements to the property so you can argue the increase in rent. Better finishes, covered parking, add an extra room or include laundry service can help increase rents, increasing the NOI and finally the value of the property.

In spite of everything we have seen, it is possible that at some point you have to sell a property either to buy a better one or for some need. In that case, do you have to pay taxes for capital gains? Of course not! A real estate investor controls their taxes and decides when and how much to pay. Let's go to the next chapter and learn to sell real estate without causing a tax event.

SUMMARY

- Instead of selling the property to make a profit and pay high taxes, you can request a loan from the bank through a refinance and you will not pay taxes for that capital.

- In no country will you be taxed if you get into debt, but on the contrary, they will give you deductions and benefits for getting into debt.

- This is what it is all about: recover your money as quickly as possible, keep the asset and obtain an infinite ROI (performance).

- Refinancing is a valid option if you are able to cover the new mortgage that your properties will have after refinancing.

- In small properties, the appreciation will generally be greater than the increase in rents.

  In large complexes, however, the appreciation will be related to the operations of the property. That is, the rents and the value of the property will increase at par, which is why there are more chances of success when refinancing in larger housing complexes (multifamily) than in individual (single family) dwellings.

- An infinite ROI is the same as saying that you are printing money. If you have an asset that pays you $ 100 a month, but you do not have any *money of your own* invested in that asset, that means that your ROI, by definition, is infinite and that you are printing money.

- The investment must make sense in a good and a bad economy.

Chapter 5

Equivalent exchange or 1031

"Buying real estate is not only the best, quickest and safest way to get rich, but the only one."

–Marshall Field

The gains obtained through equivalent exchanges are tax-free gains. In the United States, this equivalent exchange is known as *Exchange 1031*. In some countries it is also known as "reinvestments", "replacements" or "swaps". This mechanism allows an investor to move from a single-family home to departmental complexes, then to commercial properties, then buy land and return to homes again, without having to pay taxes. Some people may worry about not being able to put money in their pockets after selling their property in an equivalent exchange. This is an unfounded fear because you can always refinance the property and withdraw its appreciated value free of taxes, as we saw in the previous chapter. And even if you choose to do it, you can make another equivalent exchange later without paying taxes. It is important to know, however, that a 1031 is only available for an investment property. It does not apply for personal residence.

TAX TO CAPITAL GAINS

Capital gains only pay taxes when the last property is finally sold and a 1031 exchange is not made. How is this tax calculated? When the *tax base* of your property reaches zero, you stop receiving depreciation. At the time of selling the property, your profit is calculated as the difference between your base and your sale price. This is a basic accounting principle applicable throughout the world.

The tax base is the number used to calculate capital gains when selling a property. So it would be its formula:

Tax base: Purchase price of your property - All the depreciation you receive.

Let's see the following example to see how it works:

If you sell the property for $ 130,000, you will have a taxable gain of $ 78,000 ($ 130,000 - $ 52,000). You will basically end up paying back the deduction for depreciation (which is also known as recapture tax), in addition to the tax you pay for the increase in property value, that is, capital gains. This tax can be avoided, or rather,

Purchase price of the property	$ 100,000
Total depreciation	$48,000
Tax base for the property	$52,000
Sale price of the property	$130,000
Taxable gain	$78,000
Taxes on capital gains (20%)	$15,600

postpone, making an equivalent exchange (exchange 1031 in the United States) and defer the payment of taxes for the sale of the property. Let's see what you must do to successfully defer your taxes when selling a property.

RULES FOR A SUCCESSFUL 1031 EXCHANGE

These are the six rules you must follow to successfully postpone the payment of taxes by applying a 1031 Exchange:

1. Properties must have investment purposes, not speculation. Any type of property qualifies, as long as it is an investment property. Properties that are held for a short period of time, such as those that are repaired for resale; do not qualify for this exchange. In general, it is necessary to own both the old and the new property for not less than one year. Everything that can be classified as "real estate" qualifies for the exchange. Nor does it apply for personal residence.

2. From the day the sale of your old property is closed, you have forty-five days to provide your broker with a list of properties you would like to purchase. The forty-five days are calendar days. You will not be granted extensions for weekends. There are no limitations on properties if your list contains three of them or less. For example, you can sell a duplex for $ 100,000 and have three properties of $ 10 million each on your list, and that would be fine. But if your list has *more* than three properties, the total value of the same in the list cannot be greater than double the sale price of your old property. If our list contains four properties of $ 75,000 each ($ 300,000 in total), the entire swap is ruined. The exchange fails (even if you only purchased one of the properties) because your list

contained more than three properties and exceeded twice the sale price of your duplex (we assume you sold it for $ 100,000). The list of properties you intend to buy must be in the hands of your broker within forty-five calendar days from the time you close the sale of your old property.

3. From the day the sale of the old property is closed, you have 180 days to close the purchase of the new property. This property must be on your list that I previously gave to the forty-five-day intermediary. You can acquire one of the three properties in the list. As with the forty-five day requirement, the 180 days include weekends and holidays.

4. Make sure you choose a qualified intermediary. You are not allowed to touch the money between the sale of the old property and the purchase of the new property. The law requires you to use an independent third party, called a "qualified intermediary," to hold this money in your name. Be very careful when choosing your qualified intermediary because the law does not protect you against an intermediary of bad reputation. The intermediary is responsible for: preparing the required exchange documents and keeping the money during the exchange. Virtually everyone can play this role, except those that are related to you. Make sure the intermediary keeps your money in a separate account just for you.

5. The names of the owner (or company) that appear in the title of the old property and the title of the new one must be the same. If Robert and Melanie sold their single-family home,

then Robert and Melanie should appear in the title of the new property. They cannot put the title in the name of "real estate investments SA", because the government recognizes this company as a different taxpayer.

6. The new property that is to be purchased must have a value equal to or greater than the old property. To avoid paying taxes at the time of the exchange, you need to buy a property whose value is equal or greater and reinvest all the cash. If Robert and Melanie sell their home for $ 100,000, they must buy a new property worth at least $ 100,000 to avoid paying taxes on capital gains. If they only pay $ 90,000 for the new property, they will have to pay taxes on the $ 10,000 difference. If you are going to buy a property of $ 150,000, you sold the old one for $ 100,000 and the bank will lend you $ 100,000 for the new one, then you will only put $ 50,000, so you will pay taxes for the other $ 50,000. The option in this case would be to reduce the loan in order to invest all the capital and not pay taxes. Or you can also invest in other additional property. Of course, it must be on the forty-five day list. The new loan does not have to be the same as the previous one, only all the capital of the sale must be invested in a property of equal or greater value.

There is no limit to the number of exchanges you can make and you can continue incorporating the profits from one property to the other until you decide to take a portion of the proceeds at the time of sale. Only then you will be responsible for paying taxes. However, you must remember that *taxes do not disappear; they are only deferred until the last property is sold and not reinvested in a new one.* If you always reinvest, taxes are deferred forever. In short: *in real estate, pay taxes when you want, as you want and in the amount you want.*

COMMENTS

These indications are accurate for the United States. While they are similar in the rest of the world, they may have some changes that a qualified advisor will make you notice. This example is for educational purposes and should not be taken as a basis for making any fiscal or financial decision.

If you are a serious investor in real estate, depreciation, cost segregation, refinancing and 1031 exchange should allow you to never pay taxes on your income or sales. This is the best tax benefit in the entire tax law.

SUMMARY

- Some people may worry about not being able to put money in their pockets after selling their property in an equivalent exchange. This is an unfounded fear because you can always refinance the property and withdraw its appreciated value free of taxes, as we saw in the previous chapter. And even if you choose to do it, you can make another equivalent exchange later without paying taxes.

- A 1031 Exchange is only available for an investment property. It does not apply for personal residence or for speculation properties.

- Capital gains only pay taxes when the last property is finally sold and a 1031 exchange is not made.

- When the tax base of your property reaches zero, you stop receiving depreciation.

- At the time of selling the property, your profit is calculated as the difference between your tax base and your sale price.

- Taxes do not disappear, they are only deferred until the last property is sold and not reinvested in a new one. If you always reinvest, taxes are deferred forever. In short: in real estate, pay taxes when you want, as you want and in the amount you want.

- The indications of Exchange 1031 are accurate for the United States. While they are similar in the rest of the world, they may have some changes that a qualified advisor will make you notice.

Chapter 6
Invest through a business

I want you to take many risks.

I want you to work for free at the beginning.

No benefits. No pay.

I want you to think about me 24/7.

I cannot promise you that we will succeed.

But if we have it, I will give you everything you've always dreamed of.

-Your business

If you do not have a plan for the time when you have too much money, then most likely you will lose everything. Having a lot of money represents a problem as big as not having enough money. If you think your money problems will be solved when you have a lot of money, reality will kick you so hard that not even Google can find you. Before making money, you must have a plan. Before investing in real estate, you must have a plan. Do not invest until you have a plan. This chapter will show you the best way to invest in real estate or any other type of asset: investing through a corporation instead of investing as a natural person.

Why should you invest through a corporation? First I will tell you why you should not invest as an average person does (who is employed or self-employed): for an employee to save a thousand dollars, the government has already taken its share in advance through taxes. So as an employee or self-employed it may be necessary to earn $ 1,300 dollars just to be able to save a thousand. Then, those thousand dollars are reduced by inflation, so each year their thousand dollars are worth less. The small amount of money paid by the bank or an investment fund for interest is also reduced by inflation, as well as by taxes. That's why working hard and saving money is ridiculous. So investing as an employee or self-employed does not make much sense. The key is to become an entrepreneur and then invest.

BECOME AN ENTREPRENEUR BEFORE BECOMING AN INVESTOR

Although governments and politicians would like to charge more taxes to businesses, they realize that if they approve abusive tax laws, companies will take both their money and their jobs and leave for another country. If businessmen and investors leave a country, the economy would be destroyed because there would be no people creating jobs or actively investing in real estate.

The reason why businesses receive so many tax breaks is that the government understands that the most important function of the economy is to create jobs ... and businesses create jobs. That's why there are thousands of tax advantages for businesses and entrepreneurs. This is as true in Japan as in Colombia, Spain or the United States. And this is an important reason why the rich retain more of their wealth: for the simple fact that they act as corporate entities and not as human bodies.

Businesses are one of the best ways to reduce taxes, especially if you can turn your business into a *passive investment*. However, you should not confuse your business with your job. If your business requires that you are physically working to make it work, then it is not a business; It is a job. And in that case, you are not an entrepreneur but a self-employed person. The self-employed do not enjoy the same benefits as entrepreneurs. Entrepreneurs build businesses; the self-employed build jobs. Entrepreneurs work in the system; the self-employed work on the product. Entrepreneurs create hundreds of jobs; the self-employed create very few jobs (if they create some). For these and many more reasons is why the tax law favors employers, not the self-employed. Conversely, by turning your business into a passive investment, you can use your real estate losses that we saw in previous chapters to offset your business income. This, of course, reduces your taxes more and increases your wealth ... all with the blessing of the government.

Employees and self-employed violate the golden rule of personal finance; pay yourself first, because the government receives its share before them in the form of taxes. The bankers and the government do not have to take the money out of the employees' pockets; because that money does not even get there. It is very funny to witness how a person receives his first paycheck and see how he discovers grudgingly and surprised the difference between his gross income and his net income. As traditional education never taught him anything of this, this person believes that there is nothing he can do. But hey, at least they taught him about the mitochondria, right?

If traditional education really educates people for the real world, it would teach that the best way to invest is to have a business that buys the investments for you, and that the worst way to invest is to invest as an individual. Most people are not rich because they invest as individuals and not as business owners. The only reason to build a business is so that your business can acquire your assets. Most investments are too expensive when you acquire them as an employee or self-employed, but they are much easier to acquire if my business acquires them for me.

Remember: create businesses and get those businesses to acquire your real estate and assets.

Using a business to buy property has many benefits. Tax laws allow your business to buy real estate or other assets using pre-tax money. Is that how it works:

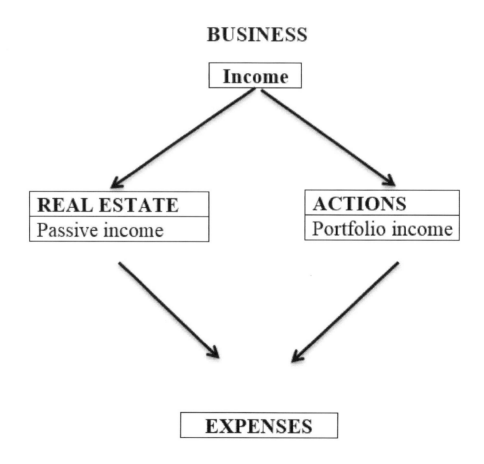

BUSINESS

In this way, businesses are able to acquire assets with money prior to paying taxes. It must be clear that the business must be an asset, and business income must be converted into more assets. Let's look at the financial status of someone who invests through a business with *pre*-tax money:

Income
Expense Acquire assets Paying taxes

On the contrary, employees try to acquire assets with the little money they have left *after* paying taxes. This would be your financial status:

Income
Expense Paying taxes Acquire assets

The rich get richer faster and more safely because they can buy assets with their *gross income*, and pay their taxes on *net income*. Employees pay their taxes on *gross* income and then try to acquire assets with their *net income*. That is why it is almost impossible for employees to achieve any kind of wealth. Employees and self-employed people provide much of their money *first* to the government, money that they could be using to buy assets. The rich pay their taxes on net income or what remains after buying assets.

This would be a summary of what happens:

Rich ⎯⎯⎯⎯➤ Acquire assets ⎯⎯⎯⎯➤ they pay taxes on what they have left.

Middle class / Poor ⎯⎯⎯➤ Pay taxes ⎯⎯⎯➤ they try to buy assets with the little money they have left.

Remember, the tax collector always gets the money first ... if you are an employee.

It is important to keep in mind that to operate in this way you necessarily need the help of professionals. A team of experts is a priority for anyone who wants to become an entrepreneur and then become an investor.

GET A TEAM OF EXPERTS

Most people who have small businesses dream of owning a Rolls Royce or a nice house someday. That's why they will never own a Rolls Royce or a big house. When you are starting, you should dream of having your own team of lawyers, accountants and tax advisors, not a German car. The problem faced by the vast majority of people is: "How to pay the expenses of a team?" It depends on how you operate. If you are an employee, the transaction would look like this:

Income
Expense Paying taxes Pay to your consultants

The transaction for entrepreneurs would look like this:

Income
Expense Pay your consultants Paying taxes

By having a legitimate business, you are allowed to deduct all expenses related to the business. You can even convert personal expenses into business expenses on many occasions.

WHICH IS THE WORLD YOU WANT TO LIVE IN?

Next let's take a look at two different worlds:

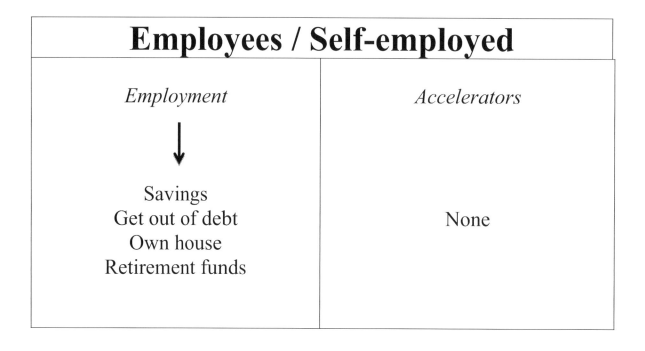

Employees / Self-employed	
Employment	*Accelerators*
↓	
Savings Get out of debt Own house Retirement funds	None

The employees do not have any accelerator, so it is almost impossible for them to get rich. The only way would be to work very hard and invest what they can discipline. This can give results, but in a very slow way.

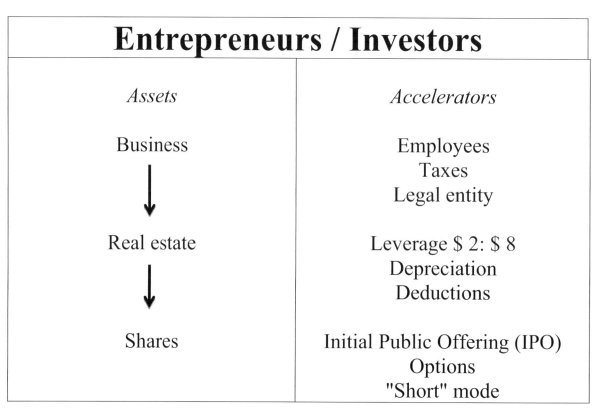

Entrepreneurs / Investors	
Assets	*Accelerators*
Business	Employees Taxes Legal entity
↓	
Real estate	Leverage $ 2: $ 8 Depreciation Deductions
↓	
Shares	Initial Public Offering (IPO) Options "Short" mode

Entrepreneurs and investors use all the possible accelerators to get rich faster and in a more secure way. They do not want to have anything in their name, since they know that this is an invitation to others to attack them. Instead, they prefer to have businesses with their respective assets and have absolute control over these businesses.

HOW TO CONVERT EARNED INCOME INTO PASSIVE INCOME

One of the advantages of being an entrepreneur and investing through a business is that you can convert the Earned Income (the income that pays more taxes) into Passive Income (the income that pays fewer taxes). Let's see an example of how it could be done:

FINANCIAL STATEMENTS

Income
Expense

Asset	Liability
My restaurant My real estate company	

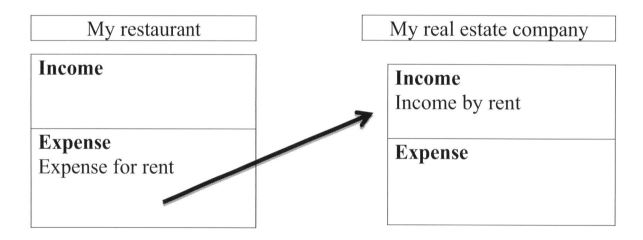

My restaurant

Income
Expense Expense for rent

My real estate company

Income Income by rent
Expense

Asset	liability

Asset	liability

The expenses go to where the control is. In this case, the restaurant business pays the rent to the real estate company.

The Earned Income of the restaurant business is being transferred and becomes the Passive Income of the real estate company. In other words, you are paying yourself. This strategy allows you to significantly reduce your taxes. The key for this to work is:

1. Have a team of expert advisors in business and real estate issues.
2. Be a legitimate businessman
3. Be a professional investor

The above example is something that Mc Donald's applies every day. The earned income earned by Mc Donald's burger business becomes passive income when it passes through Mc Donald's real estate business. If there is Mc Donald's in your city, it means that you can also apply this strategy. The key is to have business and invest through them.

IMPORTANT NOTE

You do not necessarily have to start a business to invest in real estate. While it is faster and recommended, it is not necessary. You can keep your job and follow a multi-year investment plan where you can acquire real estate, so that one day the income from these properties exceeds your salary and you can resign without problems.

You should also remember that *the important thing really is not how much money businesses make, but how much money they can invest before paying taxes.* This is what employees cannot do.

The main reason to create a business is because of the assets you can acquire before paying taxes. The laws reward businesses for investing as much money as possible. After all, it is the rich who write the rules.

SUMMARY

- If you do not have a plan for the time when you have too much money, then most likely you will lose everything.

- Become an entrepreneur before becoming an investor

- Although governments and politicians would like to charge more taxes to businesses, they realize that if they approve abusive tax laws, companies will take both their money and their jobs and leave for another country.

- The reason why businesses receive so many tax breaks is that the government understands that the most important function of the economy is to create jobs ... and businesses create jobs.

- Businesses are one of the best ways to reduce taxes, especially if you can turn your business into a passive investment.

- Employees and self-employed violate the golden rule of personal finance; *pay yourself first*, because the government receives its share before them in the form of taxes.

- Using a business to buy property has many benefits. Tax laws allow your business to buy real estate or other assets using pre-tax money.

- The rich get richer faster and more safely because they can buy assets with their *gross income*, and pay their taxes on *net income*. Employees pay their taxes on *gross* income and then try to acquire assets with their *net income*. That is why it is almost impossible for employees to achieve any kind of wealth.

- You do not necessarily have to start a business to invest in real estate.

- The important thing really is not how much money businesses earn, but how much money they can invest before paying taxes.

Epilogue

The economic system that emerged in the 20th century is completely different from the one that is commonly accepted. To this day, there is no theory of how this new system works that has a general acceptance and, in addition, there are very few who really recognize that a new system exists. The fact of having abandoned the gold standard and having embarked on the massive printing of Fiat money has changed the very nature of money and the entire global financial system.

Our civilization has been built on billions of dollars of debt, and is currently on the verge of collapse because the largest amount of that debt has been implemented in speculative activities and cannot be repaid. Because the debt is the new money, the fate that sets you apart will determine the future of the world as we know it.

The economic system that has emerged since the world adopted the Fiat money is completely new. Never in history had it been implemented on a global scale. It is a very different system from the previous one, where gold played an important role. However, something is absolutely clear: it is not a capitalist system as we know it. It is not a capitalist system because the government and the central banks manipulate the system at their whim, playing with interest rates, currencies and injecting liquidity into the market to keep them artificially standing. Capitalism was an economic system in which the private sector promoted the growth of the economy through savings, investment and inflation. The role played by the government was very limited. Currently, the government and its respective central bank create the money and manipulate its value. The current system stands up through loans and debt, not investment and savings. It is a completely different system from what people commonly imagine. A system in which the government and the central bank are the main players is not a truly capitalist system. The forces of the free market no longer move the economy. Capitalism became creditism, a system based on credit and debt that today is in a coma, on the verge of death, since it cannot bear to be injected with more debt: it has suffered a strong overdose. If our current system were really capitalist, the forces of the free market would have already collapsed it many years ago. The reality is that we still do not know for sure how it works, but its flaws have begun to be seen clearly.

It is important to recognize the following:

- The 20th century belonged to Wall Street.
- The 21st century belongs to the central banks.

If you want to keep up with what is happening and prepare for any scenario, do not listen to presidents or politicians; listen to the bankers who are in charge and look at the monetary policies they implement.

In the next years the world will realize that the dollar and all the Fiat money is a sham, and a new world order will emerge.

Note

Pirates will never make a book like this. All they do is copy, steal, alter the content and violate copyright. If you really value financial education, you want to continue learning with books like these and do not want to participate in the theft of intellectual property, keep buying these books in our social networks @Sociedadecaballeros, @ComoJugarMonopoly, @HowToPlayMonopoly and in the Amazon Kindle store. If you acquired this book by any other means, we are not responsible at all for the content you read, as it may have been altered; for the problems that you have when downloading it, since you can be a victim of cybernetic viruses; nor in case the case is presented in which your money scams you. Acquire books legally, support the unique educational content they transmit and do not support piracy.

GIFT SECTIONS

To complement your financial education, here I will present you some gift sections so that you can better understand some concepts, definitions and ideas that you should keep in mind. Some gift sections are a complement to what we are dealing with in this book and some are reviews of topics that we have already discussed in previous books.

Assets vs. Liabilities

Assets	Liabilities
They generate you money without you having to work	They cost you money
They feed you if you stop working	They eat you if you stop working
They generate a positive cash flow	They generate a negative cash flow
They make you rich	You make someone else rich
They bring you closer to financial freedom	They take you away from financial freedom at the same time that you bring someone else closer to financial freedom.

This is the difference of financial statements between the rich and the middle class:

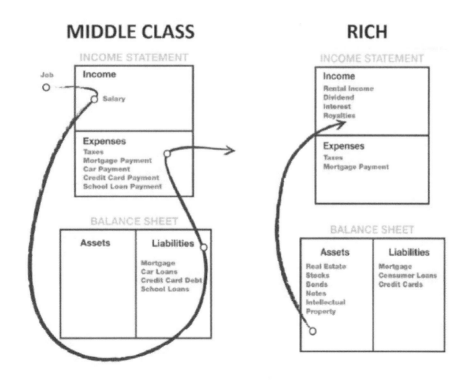

A common mistake that people make is to think that their house is an asset, but if we look carefully at the balance sheets that I show below, you will discover that your house is an asset ... but not yours.

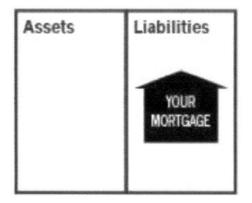
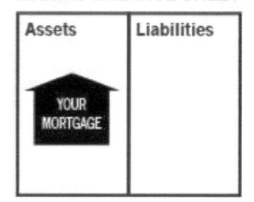

Your house is a liability because it costs you money month to month. Although it increases in value, this increase is only on paper and continues to cost you money.

Your house is not an asset of yours, but of the bank. In the end, the real asset is you, since you make the mortgage payments, insurance, services and taxes. Banks know that empty houses are liabilities. That's why they finish them off.

Even if you have already paid off the mortgage, it is still a liability for you because you still have to pay for insurance, maintenance, services and taxes. Just stop paying taxes to discover who is the real owner of your house.

What determines in the end whether something is an asset or a liability is the direction of cash flow. If cash flows inward, it is an asset. If cash flows inward, it is a liability. To acquire assets, we must know the real game of money. The game is called: ***Who owes whom?***

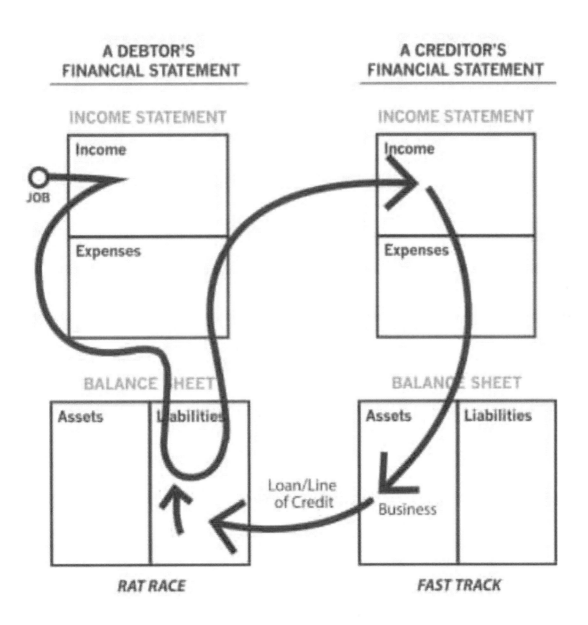

This is how the different classes play this game:

- The middle class and the poor owe them all, so their cash always flows outward.
- Everyone owes the rich, so their cash flows inward.

If you follow the cash flow, you will understand who owes whom:

1. Job → Money (Income)
2. Money (Income) → Car, house, consumption (Liabilities)
3. Car, house, consumption (Liabilities) → Expenses

This expenditure comes from the financial status of a person without financial education, and it reaches the financial status of a person with financial education, who uses that money that comes in to acquire more assets and repeat the process. It must be remembered that for each asset, there is a liability, but it does not appear in the same financial statement. The rich focus first on acquiring assets, and with those assets they can afford to acquire the liabilities they want. That's why the rich get richer.

Leverage: Less is more

These are the most common types of leverage:

1. The time of other people.
2. The money of other people.
3. The technology.
4. The education.

The leverage we work on in this book is MOP: Money from Other People, more specifically, debt. However, you must be careful, since debt is a double-edged sword.

There are basically two types of debt:

GOOD DEBT	BAD DEBT
Debt used to invest and earn a profit	Debt used to spend and lose money.
It is amortized, that is, paid by someone else.	You pay for it.
It is used to acquire assets.	It is used to acquire liabilities.
The rich use it.	It is used by the poor and the middle class.

This book focuses on teaching you how to use good debt to get enrich yourself.

Investor vs Speculator

These are the differences between a true investor and a speculator:

Investor	Speculator
Buy to conserve.	Buy to sell.
Seeks to get his money back as soon as possible, and at the same time keep retaining the asset.	Look for the price of his asset to increase to sell it and make a profit.
Buy a cow to have milk and young.	Buy a cow to kill it and sell the meat.
Look for constant cash flow.	Look for capital gains when buying low and selling high.

An investor invests in cash flow. A speculator "invests" for capital gains. Although the best word is "bet". These are the differences between cash flow and capital gains:

Cash Flow	Capital gains
What is my return on investment?	My net worth went up.
Buy a property for rent that gives me positive cash flow.	The price of my house skyrocketed.
The company's shares are paying me dividends of 72 cents per share.	I bought a house, its value increased and I sold it.
I'm going to refinance the property to recover my down payment and keep the asset.	I buy properties, I remodel them and I sell them.
My actions went up in value, but I would never sell them. I love receiving cash flow constantly.	I bought shares at $ 5 each, when they go up to $ 10, I'll sell them.
If the market collapses, I buy more properties that give me positive cash flow at a cheaper price.	If the market collapses, I lose all my inflated assets. I need it to continue to boom in order to sell more expensive in the future. I expect that there will be someone more foolish than me in the future who will buy my asset.
My wealth is my monthly cash flow.	My wealth is my net worth.

All of our books specialize in teaching you to invest by cash flow.

Types of income

Ordinary income	Passive income
It comes from a job or a punctual job.	It comes from your assets.
Your boss lends it to you.	It belongs to you.
You cannot own, sell, market, franchise or inherit it.	You can sell it or keep it. Your children and your children's children will inherit it.
It requires traditional education.	It requires financial education.
You work very hard for money.	Your money and the money of others work very hard for you.
It pays the highest taxes. Up to 50 percent	Pay the lowest taxes. Up to 0 percent
You only benefit.	You can serve more and more people.
It takes away your valuable time.	Once created, that's it. It does not take away more time. You can lie on the beach forever.
To earn more, you need to work more.	As it increases, it requires less and less physical effort.
You must work whenever you want to be paid.	You pay yourself whenever you want.
You have no control	You control everything.
It makes you a slave.	It makes you a free person.

There are basically three types of income: Ordinary, portfolio and liability. The two most important are the Ordinary Income and the Passive Income, since the Ordinary Income is the income of the great majority of the people, and the Passive Income is the income obtained by the real entrepreneurs and investors. These are its characteristics:

These incomes have a direct relationship with the following:

Cash Flow	Passive income
Capital gains	Income from capital gains or portfolio income
Employment / Savings	Ordinary income

These are some examples of how you can earn that income respectively:

Lease a property. Dividends of shares. Channel on YouTube. Licenses for books, games or intellectual property. Royalties. Marketing networks Payments for subscription to a magazine, blog or course. E-books or electronic products. Creation of apps Advertising. Vending machines	Passive income.
Speculate with a property. Speculate with shares. Resell assets. Buy and sell Bitcoins.	Income of capital gains / portfolio.
Job. Self-employment Contract for a specific job. Interest for your savings.	Ordinary income.

Formulas of a professional investor in Real Estate

- *Net Operating Income (NOI) = Revenue − Expenses.*
- *Cash flow = NOI – Mortgage.*
- *Offer price (real value) = NOI / (Capitalization rate)*
- *ROI = Profit (Cash flow) / (Initial payment) × 100*
- *(Total value of the asset - Total value of the land) / Depreciable years = Annual depreciation of the property*
- *(Total value of contents) / Depreciable years = Annual depreciation of contents*
- *Annual Total Depreciation = Annual property depreciation + Annual depreciation of the contents*

COMMENTS:

- Capitalization rates are determined by evaluating recent sales statistics of similar properties in a given market. A real estate broker will provide you with this information.
- The NOI is the first and most important indicator of a property. However, do not get too excited when you see a high NOI. It is simply an indicator of the cash flow of the property and does not include mortgage payments. The mortgage payments will depend on the purchase price, the initial payment and the interest rate.
- The offer price is based on the operations of the property and the capitalization rate that your broker gives you. This price

you find is the most you will pay for the property. You should always keep in mind that the value of the property is NEVER determined by the sale price. The real value of the property for an investor is based on its operations. It's easier to negotiate with the seller when you have numbers that support your offer.

- You must be careful with the deduction for depreciation. Understanding taxes and tax advantages does not mean you can apply them yourself. Unless you are a Certified Public Accountant (CPA), look for a competent one and work with him. You must also take care of incompetent advisors. Many accountants and lawyers are afraid of being strong by applying these deductions. Make sure you have consultants on your team who have experience working on these issues, mainly with entrepreneurs and investors. You would be surprised to discover how many Accountants and Tax Advisors are unaware of these advantages and cost their clients millions.

- Keep in mind that the years that you can depreciate the properties and contents vary in each country. For purposes of simplifying this book, we take the years that can be depreciated residential properties in the United States, i.e., 27.5 years or 3.6% per year of the value of the building and the corresponding percentage for commercial properties, which is 2.5% per year. Remember that the contents can depreciate much faster, sometimes up to 20% per year, increasing your deductions and therefore your cash flow. Work with your advisor to see how this applies to your investments since each situation is unique.

- All the examples contained throughout the course are for educational purposes and you should not take them as a basis for making any financial decision. Taxes can be a complex issue that changes constantly, and unless you want to end up in trouble or be audited, it is best to strive to find the best possible advisor and work with him.

To better understand all these formulas, read ***How to play Monopoly in the real world,*** where we explain with step-by-step examples the main function of the NOI and the capitalization rate.

Assets that protect against hyperinflation

There is a formula that serves to protect against inflation and is summarized in five words: *Play the game of the bank*. By borrowing money from the bank at a *fixed rate*, acquire a property that generates cash flow and put as little money as possible, you will recover your money faster and your performance will be higher.

In an inflationary economy (the one that all countries currently live), if the payment of the debt you acquired to invest in an asset is *fixed*, it becomes cheaper as money loses its value as inflation increases. In this way, every time you pay less money for the debt you acquired (since the rate is fixed and the purchasing power of all currencies is in decline) and every time you earn more money since you have more and you can raise the income to the same rhythm that increases inflation.

While the interest rate on debt remains fixed, real estate income usually increases with inflation.

The reason why the rich get richer is because they acquire assets that adjust to inflation (real estate) and use borrowed money to acquire them at a fixed rate. Money is worth less and less because of inflation, so they pay less and less for these loans every time, and their assets as real estate are worth more, again due to inflation.

This is valid for all the capitalist countries of the world.

The system is designed to make the poor poorer, the middle class to work increasingly less and less, and the rich to become richer by using debt, taxes and inflation, all in a legal manner.

In the previous periods of very high inflation or hyperinflation, debtors and speculators have come out as winners at the expense of those who had savings. When hyperinflation occurs, the currency is losing all or almost all of its value against other currencies. Therefore, speculators get rich betting against the currency that is sinking (selling short). And on the other hand, debtors are enriched due to their ability to borrow at fixed interest rates. Debtors benefit when prices rise because their income increases, but the amount of debt they owe remains constant. Therefore, it is easier for them to return it. In periods of high inflation or hyperinflation, the debt practically disappears. That process hurts creditors and savers. Hyperinflation can completely evaporate the savings of anyone who does not have enough financial education to transfer their wealth to real assets. This is one of the safest ways to get rich during a period of high inflation.

Remember: you can only use inflation to enrich yourself if you use debt to acquire assets that generate cash flow.

Assets that protect against deflation

Extreme inflation is like fire, in the sense that it consumes people's savings. Extreme deflation is like ice, in the sense that it leaves the frozen economy in a shortage of liquidity with high unemployment and without any growth. Both would end up leaving the economy in a scenario of disaster and chaos. However, each affects the price of the assets in a different way.

In a deflation (at least one not so high) those who have large amounts of gold or cash would be in a very advantageous position to buy real estate and other real assets at auction prices. Those who have these real assets would realize that they are in a much better position than those who have nothing assets. However, in a serious debt deflation almost everyone would lose, since the financial system would collapse as a result of bankruptcies and massive defaults. In addition, with the social upheaval that would probably begin, it is not entirely clear if property rights would continue to be respected. Forced redistribution of land and property may take place. For this reason, central banks and governments are determined to do whatever is necessary to prevent this from happening, even if that means printing massive amounts of money and taking us on the path of high inflation.

The global financial system is sick. It is not known how much longer he can survive. What determines the cause of his death will be the policy taken by central banks and governments. If indebtedness stops and expenditure is not stimulated, the system will die because of deflation. If the debt continues to increase, too much is spent and Fiat money is printed in excess, inflation will be very high or we could even experience hyperinflation as in Venezuela, with all the consequences that entails.

By abandoning the gold standard and implementing a financial system based on Fiat money, the following should be clear for the future: *there is no scenario in which gold and silver do not rise in price.* While paper money continues to be devalued due to central bank policies, gold and silver will continue to be the best shelters to protect against any future scenario.

Do not waste a recession

If you see a pair of expensive shoes that you love with a 50% discount, I'm sure you would buy them immediately.

Think of a recession as a season of discounts where you can buy assets at half price.

$ 10,000 dollars invested in Amazon 17 years ago would be worth $ 2,065,734 today! Imagine having a second chance to buy at that price. The same applies to real estate and other types of assets.

So remember: when all the other amateurs are selling, you should think about buying.

"Be fearful when others are greedy and be greedy when others are fearful."

–Warren Buffett

Questions to a tax advisor

Your taxes to pay depend more on the tax advisor you choose than on anything else. However, the person who advises you can only be as smart as you are. If you do not know much, they cannot tell you much. If you want to receive sophisticated advice, you must be a sophisticated investor. If you are like the average person who works hard at a job and saves money, you cannot expect to receive high quality advice. Remember: if your personal situation changes, your taxes change. Here are some questions you can ask a tax advisor to see if you are able to give you the best possible advice:

1. What do you think of the tax law?
2. Who benefits most from the tax law?
3. Why did you become a tax advisor?
4. What would you like to know about me?
5. Tell me about your advisory team.
6. Describe your business experience
7. What is your personal investment strategy?
8. Give me three examples of how you would reduce my risk of being audited.
9. What do you think about asset protection?

In the end, the important thing is not how much your tax advisor *charges* you, but how much it *costs* you.

Glossary

Asset: Anything that puts money in your pocket without you having to work physically.

Leverage: Buy or invest with borrowed money.

Appreciation: Increase in the value of an asset over time. It can occur for several reasons: devaluation of the currency, increase in demand, changes in inflation or fluctuations in the interest rate. It applies to any type of asset.

Duty: Tax that must be paid on imported or exported products.

Speculative attack: Take down the shares of a company or the currency of a particular country through huge sales in short, with the aim of obtaining quick profits or to achieve a corporate take.

Bankruptcy: Not be able to pay debts or have excess liabilities in relation to the market value of the assets that are owned.

Central bank: A bank that may or may not be part of the government, which controls the money supply of a country. It has the power to issue the notes of a country, regulate commercial banks, manipulate interest rates and do whatever is necessary to protect the economy.

Investment bank: A bank that issues securities and sells them to investors. It is characterized by managing assets, negotiating securities and providing advice to its clients. They differ from commercial banks in that they do not receive deposits or make commercial loans, although after the repeal of the *Glass Steagall* Act in 1999, which prohibited the same bank from taking deposits and placing securities, the issue and operations have become confusing that these banks really manage. *Morgan Stanley, Goldman Sachs and Merill Lynch* are the main investment banks.

Real estate: Real estate properties such as buildings, warehouses, commercial premises, land, etc.

Bubble: An exaggerated and illusory rise in the price of an asset, which is largely out of proportion to the value of the underlying asset. In the tulip bubble in Holland, with a single tulip you could buy a house in front of the Amsterdam canal. This is an example of a bubble, where the price of a tulip, which represents the "active" in this case, goes up dramatically.

Capitalist: Entrepreneur or investor who creates jobs, affordable housing, commerce, investment opportunities and keeps the economy afloat.

Capitalization: Market value of the shares of a company.

Credit Risk Coverage (CRC for its acronym in English): Contracts that are sold as protection against defaults in the payment of loans, similar to insurance, except that no insurance regulator verifies that the "seller of the protection "(Which is usually a Coverage Fund) can fulfill its promise in the event of a default in payment. Basically, a CRC is a bet, where the "protection seller" agrees to pay if the underlying credit instrument enters into default, and the "buyer of the protection" agrees to pay a premium for it.

Commodities: Tangible items such as gold, silver, oil, gas and livestock.

Variable Rate Mortgage Credit (VRMC): Mortgage loan in which the interest rate and payments are adjusted frequently. The purpose of this loan is to allow mortgage interest rates to fluctuate with market conditions.

Deflation: Contraction in the supply of money or credit, which causes a decrease in prices; the opposite of inflation.

Depositary: Bank that keeps funds deposited by others and facilitates the exchange of same.

Depreciation: Method of assigning the cost of a tangible asset over its useful life. In real estate, it is a deduction from the income tax that allows a taxpayer to recover its cost or its base from a certain property. It can be applied even if the property is increasing in value in the market. It is an annual subsidy that an investor receives for the deterioration, deterioration or obsolescence of the property. Only the deduction for depreciation applies to investors. It does not apply to speculators or owners of your own home who want to depreciate your home.

Derivative: Financial instrument whose price is derived from one or more underlying assets. Example: Apple shares depend on the company Apple Computers. The "futures" and the options are derivatives.

Good debt: Debt used to acquire assets that generate cash flow and that is amortized, that is, paid by someone else.

Bad Debt: Debt that is used to acquire liabilities that generate an expenditure of money and that is paid from one's own pocket.

Commodity money: Money that has intrinsic value, such as gold or silver.

Receipt money: Paper money that represents a real asset, such as gold or silver.

Fiat Money: Legal tender paper that is not backed and cannot be converted into gold or silver.

Multiplier effect: The monetary expansion of a country, resulting from the ability of banks to grant loans.

Entrepreneurs: People who take risks in order to solve a problem and create a business system around.

Ponzi scheme: Pyramid in which the investor is paid with the money of later investors.

Financial statement: Shows how cash flows between the balance sheet (assets and liabilities) and the income statement (income and expenses).

Cash flow: Money that comes from an asset and that you earn to work or not.

Hedge Funds: Investment companies that use high-risk techniques, such as borrowing money and selling short, in order to earn high returns for their investors.

Capital gains: This is the way most people invest. Basically it is "buy cheap and sell expensive". It is very similar to betting. For this reason, people believe that investing is risky. It is speculating that the value of the investment will increase over time, something that could happen or not.

Deficit spending: Excess of spending by the government compared to what it earns.

Hyperinflation: Period in which the currency of a country loses all its value. When it happens, people who work for money and save it (employees) end up losing everything and become part of the lower class.

Mortgage: Loan to finance the purchase of real estate, usually with specific periods of payment and interest.

Inflation: Persistent increase in the level of consumer prices (CPI), either by an artificial increase in the money supply or a speculative attack on the currency. In both cases, what causes inflation mainly is the devaluation of the currency. In the first case, inflation occurs only if the money supply grows beyond the proportion of products and services, that is, when there is more and more money to buy the same products and services.

Earned income (salary or payroll check): Money earned in a job and usually called a "payroll check". It is also called "salary", "commission" or "rate". It is the income that pays the most taxes in the whole world and it occurs when a person works very hard in exchange for money.

Portfolio income (capital gains): Most amateur investors only know this type of income and it occurs when buying cheap and selling expensive. Pay between 10-25% taxes depending on the country and the circumstance.

Passive income (cash flow): It is an income that pays very few taxes, or even none. It occurs in the form of income, royalties, dividends and other forms of cash flow. Its money that comes to you periodically, work or not.

Compound interest: Interest calculated not only on the initial capital but on the accumulated interest of previous payment periods.

Fundamental investment: Analyze financial statements, profits, the management team and the potential of a long-term asset. The numbers are your friends.

Technical investment: Analyze market feeling at a given time and trends that are caused by buyers and sellers. The trend is your friend.

Free trade: Trade between nations where there is no restriction of any kind (import tariffs, export refunds, etc.). Generally, in the more developed nations, free trade ends up causing jobs to be exported abroad, where labor costs are lower. On the other hand, in less developed nations, employees and the environment are exploited by foreign financiers, who take control of labor and natural resources in exchange for money.

Margin: When an investor buys "on the sidelines", he is investing with borrowed money. The loan is made by a commission agent, who will be paid with the profits made by the investor when his investment is appreciated. If the investment loses its value, the investor would record a loss and run the risk of not being able to repay his loan.

Stock market: A system through which the shares of several companies are sold to the public, offering them the opportunity to participate in the success of the same.

Currency: Money in any of its forms, which is used as a means of exchange accepted by the public.

Currency of legal tender (money by decree): Money that legally must be accepted because a government law indicates it.

Monetize: Convert government debt in the form of securities (bonds, notes, bills), to money that can be used to purchase products and services.

Collateralized Debt Obligations (CDO): Complex financial instruments that unite and separate individual loans into products that can be sold in the stock market. These packages are made up of vehicle loans, credit card debts or corporate debts. They are called "collateralized" because they have some kind of collateral behind them. They are sold as if they were protected against failures or defaults, with risky bets called "derivatives".

Monetary offer: Total amount of bills, coins, loans, credits and other liquid instruments in the economy of a country.

Oligarchy: Government led by a few members of the elite.

Gold standard: Monetary system in which the currency is convertible to fixed amounts of gold.

Liabilities: Anything that makes you lose money. Your house, your car, and your credit cards are usually the clearest examples.

Plutocracy: Form of government in which power falls on the hands of those who have more money; government of the rich.

Reflation: Intentional reversal of deflation, through monetary actions by the government or central bank.

Federal Reserve: The central bank of the United States in charge of regulating the money supply of the country. Despite what is believed, it is not a government entity; it is privately owned and pays dividends to its shareholders.

Moral risk: Risk that the existence of a contract may change the way in which the parties act in the future. For example, if your home is insured against fire, you will take fewer precautions against such an event. If the banks are insured against their own insolvency and fraudulent loans, they will not be careful when engaging in speculative or fraudulent activities.

Wealth: When your passive income and portfolio income exceed your expenses, you will be free financially.

Fluctuating exchange rate: Foreign exchange rate, which is not set by national authorities, but varies depending on supply and demand.

Title: A transferable interest rate representing financial value; an investment instrument issued by a corporation, government or other organization that offers evidence of a debt or participation.

Usury: The practice of lending money and charging interest to the borrower, especially at an exorbitant or illegal rate.

Short sale: Borrow a title or value and sell it in the hope of buying it back cheaper later, before having to pay the lender. A naked short sale is a short sale in which the seller does not buy shares to replace those he has borrowed.

The best of our blog

The best financial education blog you will find it by accessing our website https://how2playmonopoly.com/blogs-2/ Make sure you create an account and review it regularly. Do not miss anything! Here I will show you our best blogs.

MC BILLIONARY: REAL ESTATE = WEALTH

Ray Kroc did not found **Mc Donald's**, but he was the one who turned it into a multi-billion dollar business.

He started selling franchises earning 1.9% of each sale. Since it was earned income (the income that pays more taxes), he barely had enough to cover the expenses and although he had many franchises, this model was not profitable.

Ray realized that buying the land where the franchises were and leasing them, he made a lot more money.

In this way, he converted the income earned from the hamburger business, to passive income in the real estate business.

He bought Mc Donald's rights to the founders for $ 2.7 million and the rest is history.

Mc Donald's business is real estate. Ray Kroc knew the formula of the rich:

Real estate = Wealth

If you understand the real estate business, you understand why McDonald's pays 0% in taxes.

Let's say the hamburger business gets $ 1 million of earned income.

Now let's say that the real estate business has $ 1 million in depreciation of its real estate.

The million in earned income from hamburgers is offset by the million in depreciation of the real estate business.

The final result is that it pays zero taxes.

If Mc Donald's did not have real estate, he would pay more than $ 450,000 in taxes for his million earned income.

Do not worry if you do not understand. Neither your professor with a doctorate will understand. That's why the rich get richer while your teacher works for a payroll check.

REAL ESTATE: THE PARADISE OF THE RICH

Debt and taxes can make you very poor ... except in real estate.

Real estate is the "printing press" of the rich.

For example, let's suppose you have $ 20,000 to invest. If you acquire property by leveraging money from banks, you can end up acquiring assets worth up to $ 100,000, assuming 80% financial leverage.

Let's suppose that your new investment is valued after a few years and is now worth $ 120,000. How can you take this money, keep the asset, reinvest in another property and repeat the process, all at the same time?

Two words: debt and taxes.

If you apply a refinance for the new value of the property (debt), you get the surplus value as tax-free money. Next, the new debt is amortized by the tenant, you reinvest that money by applying an "equivalent exchange" (exchange 1031 as it is known in the United States), which means that you do not pay taxes for capital gains, as long as you comply some requirements and buy another investment property, and you re-leverage with the bank's money (without paying taxes).

All the debt you have is making you richer, since you do not pay for it: your tenant pays and you have a profit.

This is a very sophisticated investment method that is done all over the world.

It sounds simple, but in practice it is much more complex.

You need a high financial education to operate in this way.

You do not need a diploma, a lot of money or being a financial genius. Anyone with a financial education can play a monopoly in the real world if they know the methods.

In our guide to investing *How to play monopoly in the real world* I will show you step by step how to do it.

THE BEST EMPLOYEE MEETS THE BEST ENTREPRENEUR

In 2010, when Steve Jobs was fighting against cancer, he met with the president of the United States at the time, Barack Obama, for 45 minutes. Below are fragments from Walter Issacson's free, Steve Jobs: "The administration should be more perceptive when it comes to business. Steve described how easy it was to build a factory in China and I said that in the United States it was almost impossible because of regulations and high costs. "

"Jobs attacked the education system; He mentioned that it was too old-fashioned and that it was damaged by the rules of the unions. Until the unions disappeared, there would be almost no hope of educational reform. Teachers should be treated as professionals, he said, not as workers in an assembly line. Directors should be able to hire and fire them based on their performance. "

"It is absurd," he added, "that the classrooms still function with teachers standing next to a blackboard and textbooks. All books, advisory and learning materials should be digital and interactive, designed according to the needs of each student, and capable of providing feedback in real time.

Thanks Steve.

Robots are displacing workers, jobs are moving to emerging economies, automation is eliminating millions and millions of jobs, world currencies are constantly being devalued by the massive printing of money from central banks, the bet of Wall Street with derivatives is causing worldwide explosions, the pension and retirement system around the world is broken and it is a time bomb that exploded stronger than subprime mortgages, and countries like Greece, Spain, Italy, Portugal, Ireland, Venezuela and many more are bankrupt and may never recover.

The crisis we are going through and that will increase in these times is not financial: it is educational. All this is the cause of the obsolete educational system.

The best employee, Barack Obama, believes in giving people fish by raising taxes and creating more subsidies.

The best businessman, Steve Jobs, believes in teaching people how to fish by implementing an educational reform that leads to the obsolete educational system of the industrial age, to the information age.

WHAT DO THE MONKEYS PREFER?

"If you put bananas and money in front of the monkeys, the monkeys will choose the bananas because they do not know that the money can buy many bananas.

*In the real world, if you offer **EMPLOYMENT** and **BUSINESSES** to people, the majority will always be inclined to a job because they have no idea that businesses can bring much more money than payroll checks.*

Businesses and investments generate passive income, and these are much better than wages, since wages can give you a life, but passive income can give you a fortune. "

-Jack Ma, founder of Alibaba and the richest man in China.

The school teaches people to be monkeys. It teaches them how to look for a safe job, a small payroll check and encourages people to save money and get out of debt. The problem with these tips is that they are for average people, and average people drive a Toyota, have 2 weeks of vacation a year and work very hard all their lives. If that's what you want, then get a job and do what the school teaches.

But if you do not want to be a monkey that is limited to obeying orders and never questioning the status quo, then traditional education is not for you.

If only people knew that passive income is better than payroll checks there would be fewer "monkeys" asking for jobs, raises and subsidies and more entrepreneurs creating new products, trade and innovative investments.

The school makes monkeys ... and that is the root of the whole problem.

A MUGGING CALLED EDUCATION

The education system is not meant to help people become smart, but to prevent them from being smart. There is a stupid form of erudition. In addition, in kindergarten to university, it can be a way of being a scholar, a way of being mediocre and another, because education must be repeated. That is the criterion used to judge his intelligence.

That may be the criterion for judging parrot's memory, but that is not an intelligence criterion. Intelligence is a totally different phenomenon. Intelligence has nothing to do with repetition; in fact, intelligence hates repetition. Intelligence will always try to live life in its own way. Intelligence will always want to do its own things. The intelligence will want to deepen into the mysteries of life without following a series of pre-established formulas or strategies; Intelligence is always original.

Universities do not allow for intelligent people. Exclude the original people; all their effort consists in destroying originality, because original people will always create problems for society. They will not be so easy to manipulate, and it will not be so easy to reduce them to be school employees and teachers; It will not be easy to reduce them to be efficient machines. They will affirm themselves, they will try to live life not according to a pattern, but according to their own understanding.

WHAT IS A SOCIALIST?

One day, a socialist went to a farmer's house to try to convince him of the socialist ideology.

- "What does it mean to be a socialist?" Asked the farmer.

- "It means that if you have a tree, then we can all benefit from its fruits," the Socialist replied.

- "That sounds really good. Tell me more. "

- "Well, if you have a crop, we can all benefit from the harvest."

- "Wow! Being a socialist is something incredible! "Replied the farmer.

Following the same logic, the socialist said: "Also, if you have a cow, we can all benefit from milk."

- "What!? Get out of my property and take all your socialist ideas away from here! "Replied the angry farmer.

The socialist, very confused, asked the farmer: "I do not understand. Why was it good for him to share his fruits and his harvest, but not the milk of the cow? "

"Because I do not have trees that give fruits and I do not cultivate anything in my lands, but I do have cows that give milk!"

That's what socialism is about. Everyone wants to share and share things equally ... as long as it's not theirs!

In socialism, dictators and politicians become rich.

In capitalism, entrepreneurs and investors become rich.

The Bible explains both concepts better: "Give a man a fish, and feed him for a day. Teach him how to fish, and you will feed him all his life. "It's time to teach people how to fish.

WHY DOES NOT DONALD TRUMP PAY TAXES?

Do you see your salary every month asking where all your money is going? I'll tell you. It goes to people who know how to use taxes to create money instead of losing it.

During the last presidential campaign in the United States, President Trump was involved in a lot of controversy when he said: "I do not pay taxes." Many people got upset and called him a cheat or a thief. What average people do not understand, is that Trump is doing exactly what the government needs done.

Every country needs entrepreneurs and investors. The tax laws will reward these people and create jobs and affordable housing. After all, that is what creates a great economy.

If the government needs more low-cost houses, they will give a good fiscal incentive to motivate developers to create affordable homes. If the government needs to create jobs, they will give a good fiscal incentive to entrepreneurs who start a business and create jobs. The problem is that the government still has to pay its bills. So, to whom do you charge taxes? To the middle class. And they use those taxes to subsidize entrepreneurs and investors who behave as they want to receive tax benefits.

The foundations of the fiscal law are practically the same in all the capitalist countries. It is businessmen and professional investors who get all the tax benefits.

You might think that you have no choice about how much taxes you pay. Everyone has to pay taxes, right? Lie. There are a lot of people who pay little or nothing taxes legally.

How to do what the rich do? Buy assets and use borrowed money to buy those assets.

For example, when buying a property using money from the bank, the tenant pays the debt, and in addition, there is a profit that goes to your pocket. When you operate like this, this is what happens:

1. You receive a tax benefit for incentivizing the economy by borrowing.
2. You provide housing for people who cannot buy their own house.
3. You use financial leverage.
4. You create cash flow.

Paying fewer taxes is totally legal in all countries. If you are a serious businessman or investor, the tax code is on your side.

Was the law written for the rich? Of course!

CONGRATULATIONS! YOU ARE A BILLIONAIRE!

It is not very difficult to be a billionaire at present. In fact, in just five minutes you can get it. Do you want me to tell you the secret? All you have to do is go online and buy a one-billion-dollar Zimbabwean bill. So you can tell your friends: "I'm a billionaire." You would be, of course, but you would also be bankrupt. Probably, with that ticket you reach to buy an egg. Sure, if you find someone who is willing to sell you.

The big trap in the modern economy is money. Excess of money virtually all people graduate and immediately fall into the trap: they get a job, work hard for money and make an effort to save it.

It all started in 1971. That was the year that people who work for money and save it became the biggest losers in the modern economy. Richard Nixon broke the Bretton Woods Agreement with the world, ceasing to back the dollar with gold. So that the other countries could continue belonging to the club, the International Monetary Fund and the World Bank demanded that they do the same. From then on, countries and central banks began to print money out of nowhere and every time the United States needed money, it only turned on the printing press and began to print toy money.

Why is it so important that a currency be backed by gold or silver? Because without the discipline that gold provides, central banks and governments embark on a process known as "systematic inflation." They create money out of nowhere, they give it to their bankers friends, they increase inflation, debt and taxes, and of course, they destroy the purchasing power of the currency in question. That's why savers are losers. This system will survive as long as the world follows the flow to the big heist, but if people wake up from the fantasy in which they live submerged, from that belief that they can buy things with toy money, then the scheme will collapse and we will go into depression ... a new depression caused by inflation. The hyperinflation in Zimbabwe and Venezuela are just a few glimpses into the future that awaits us: the total and permanent death of paper money.

In the next years it will be discovered that modern money is a fraud and a new global economy will emerge. Throughout history, whenever the money is left behind with a precious metal ends up returning to its original value: zero. It already happened, and not only in Zimbabwe and Venezuela, but in the United States and Germany.

The true winners of the modern economy will be those who understand that the money they have in their wallet does not belong to them, and that the wisest thing is to acquire assets that generate cash flow and adjust to inflation.

THE FINAL JUDGMENT OF UNCLE SAM

The reason why the United States is such a rich country nowadays is because it can pay its debts and trade with dollars that they have printed, that is, legalized false money. If Argentina or any other country had its currency as a world reserve, it would also be a rich country. The danger is that if the dollar loses too much credibility, countries like China could create a new reserve currency. If that happens, the United States would be annihilated. I could not live on fake money any longer.

If the dollar is dethroned as a world reserve currency, foreign investors and central banks will no longer have any interest in having US dollars. They will be sent back to the United States, where they came from. Billions of them will return to their home, after a vacation in the vaults of foreign countries, now ready to destroy the domestic economy.

These dollars will start buying televisions, cars, appliances, computers, factories, real estate, office buildings, cargo ships and many other products, making prices rise to unimaginable levels just a year ago.

The United States will finally experience the hyperinflation that it had to experience many years ago but that was postponed because the other countries were very kind enough to accept taking those counterfeit dollars away and exchanging them for their products.

When everything collapses, it will be because to date the United States has the power to finance its trade deficit with Fiat money created from out of nowhere by the Federal Reserve. If this could not be done, the trade deficit would not exist.

The United States can falsify money and trade with everyone because it is in the unique position of having its currency accepted as a means of international trade (petrodollars). Thanks to that, you can create Fiat money out of nowhere, and the other countries have no choice but to accept it. In this way the United States has been able to spend much more than it earns because the Fed can create all the money it needs.

All countries that have refused to accept dollars have been invaded or destabilized. The problem is that the US cannot invade countries like Russia or China as it can do with Iran and Syria.

The United States has achieved a feat that no other nation has ever been able to achieve in history: trade with everyone with monopoly money printed exclusively for Uncle Sam's use.

But if China or Russia comes to the party and take the guests, USA would have its days numbered.

WELCOME TO WONDERLAND

It is the central banks, not the government, that produces all the paper money and lends it to the government and private institutions with interests. That's why public debt is out of control.

Possibly now you would ask yourself: "If we pay all the currency that was asked to create the monetary supply but we still owe the interest, where are we going to get the currencies to pay these interests to the central banks if these same ones create the currencies of the nothing?"

Answer: we have to borrow it again for it to exist. This is the reason why public debt continues expanding: because it can never be paid. It is mathematically impossible.

When you or I issue a check, there must be enough funds in our account to back it up, but when a central bank like the Fed issues a check, there is no bank deposit against which the document can be changed. When the Fed issues a check, it is making money, or in reality, currency. And in fact those dollars of recent manufacture are deposited in the banks, they apply another trick of magic: the fractional bank reserve, that is, they create more money out of nowhere.

This is the trick: banks do not actually lend the currencies that are in the accounts. Instead, they create new bills by decree, take them out of nowhere and then lend them, which means that they also "borrow" to be able to exist.

In a nutshell:

- We have borrowed each ticket for it to exist, since the central banks were created.
- We pay interest for each ticket that exists.
- That interest is paid to the central banks, which are private banks.
- The largest banks in the world are the owners of the Fed, not the government.
- The United States mathematically cannot pay off its debt ... it can only keep asking for more to pay interest.
- The income tax was created to pay these interests.

Welcome to Wonderland.

THE RAT RACE

If we follow the life of the average person, with average education, it will look a lot like the following:

The person goes to school, graduates, finds a secure job and soon has some extra money to spend. Now this person can pay the rent of an apartment, buy a television, new clothes, some furniture and of course, a new car. And the accounts begin to arrive. One day, meet someone special, fly sparks, fall in love and get married. For some time life is wonderful because two can live on one's salary. Now they have two incomes, a single rent to pay and they can set aside a few dollars to buy the dream of all the young couples: their own house. They find the house they dream of, they withdraw the money from the savings account and they use it to give the initial payment of the house and now they have a mortgage. Because they have a new home, they need new furniture, so they find a furniture store that advertises their products with the magic words: "No down payment. Easy monthly payments. "

Life becomes wonderful and they offer a party for all their friends to know their new home, their new car, their new furniture and their new toys. Now, without realizing it, they are indebted for the rest of their lives. And then the first child arrives.

The average couple, with a university education and a worker, after leaving the child in daycare, they should now work very hard. They have been trapped by the need to have a secure job simply because, on average, they are only three months away from total bankruptcy.

The couple believes that their problem is lack of money, so they work even harder and get an increase or a part-time job. Immediately he earns more money, the following happens: he pays more taxes, he works more, he has less free time and his debts increase. This couple begins to resemble the rats that are seen in stores: no matter how hard they try, they will keep going around and around without ever getting anywhere.

You can listen to these people, as they often say: "I cannot quit my job, I have many bills to pay", or "I cannot afford it, I have a family to support".

Working for money is a trap ... a trap so subtle that millions of people fall into it every day.

About us.

Our mission is to provide people with the knowledge that schools and universities did not consider important, but that is the basis of every successful entrepreneur and investor.

In these times of financial uncertainty, market collapses, depressed economies, unstable employment, constant devaluation of the purchasing power of money and bankrupt governments, financial education is the only weapon available to the average citizen.

Our social networks, blogs, books and courses aim to prepare and educate as many people as possible who want to become entrepreneurs and investors, with knowledge that can be applied in the real world.

If you want to know more about our courses and educational material we have for you, enter our social networks or our website and ask us.

The courses we will have and all our educational material is designed so that it is available to everyone, so it will always be digital, and the knowledge can be learned and applied by all people, regardless of their academic or economic level. Our educational material is designed and designed to be the best learning of your life.

I hope to meet you some day and tell me your success story. It has been a real privilege to spend this time with you. We will meet soon!

A hug.

Santiago R. T

Books by the same author

These are the current books and the courses belonging to the same author, to @Sociedadecaballeros, to @ComoJugarMonopolio and @HowToPlayMonopoly:

SANTIAGO R. T.

HOW TO PLAY MONOPOLY IN THE REAL WORLD

Why the rent of a green house is better than a paycheck

HOW TO PLAY MONOPOLY IN THE REAL WORLD

Why renting a green house is better than a payroll check

- ✓ How money and central banks work in the world.
- ✓ How to read financial statements.
- ✓ The difference between assets and liabilities.
- ✓ Why savers are losers.
- ✓ How to use debt to get rich.
- ✓ The difference between an investor and a speculator.
- ✓ How to earn several types of passive income.
- ✓ How to analyze properties step by step.
- ✓ How to put together a team of specialists and what to expect from each member.
- ✓ A technique to know what property to buy, how much to pay for this and how much profitability to expect. The risk is almost zero if you apply this methodology.
- ✓ How can you manage a property.
- ✓ Everything you need to know to close the deal and sleep peacefully at night.
- ✓ How to make yourself rich by taking advantage of a recession.
- ✓ Tips for you to start a successful business.

✓ Habits that when applied every day will change your life.
✓ What all the millionaires do that others cannot imagine.
✓ How to move forward and overcome everything.

… And much more.

SANTIAGO R. T.

HOW TO MAKE $50,000 IN SOCIAL MEDIA

Learn how to make 100K followers and $50,000 in social media

HOW TO EARN $ 50,000 DOLLARS IN SOCIAL NETWORKS

Learn to earn 100K followers and $ 50,000 in less than six months with little money

In this book I will show you the secrets of social networks and the steps I followed to create two brands on Instagram, Facebook, Snapchat and Twitter with more than 150,000 followers and a profit of more than $ 50,000 in less than six months by investing only $ 300 Dollars.

I will teach you the following:

- ✓ How to earn money through social networks without investing money.
- ✓ How to become an authentic influencer.
- ✓ How to create a brand in social networks from the start.
- ✓ Step by step guide to start.
- ✓ How to automate your social networks.
- ✓ You will know the secrets of Instagram.
- ✓ The most important treasure of social networks.
- ✓ Quick guide to start winning followers.
- ✓ How to make a marketing campaign to gain 15k followers in 1 week.
- ✓ How to make an email marketing campaign.
- ✓ How to use WhatsApp to sell.

✓ Ideas to earn money through social networks.
✓ How to sell anything.

SANTIAGO R. T.

HOW TO BECOME A BUSINESS OWNER

Learn how to build a business step by step and raise capital.

HOW TO BECOME A BUSINESS OWNER

Learn to build a successful business step by step and raise capital

This unpublished material is what you were waiting for. Let me show you what you will find in this book:

- ✓ How to build a business.
- ✓ How to raise capital.
- ✓ How to present a business to an investor.
- ✓ How to know and analyze the numbers of a business.
- ✓ Directory of investors in Latin America.
- ✓ How to move from an idea to a successful and automated business.
- ✓ How to sell.
- ✓ How to manage and train your business team.
- ✓ How to deal with venture capital investors.
- ✓ The 7 phases of all entrepreneurship.
- ✓ How to analyze the feasibility of an idea.
- ✓ How to boost your business with social networks.

…and much more.

HOW TO MAKE MONEY FROM SCRATCH

Let me show you everything you will learn in this course:

- ✓ How to generate income without money.
- ✓ How to make Amazon your best partner.
- ✓ How to take advantage of all the business modalities in Amazon.
- ✓ Why sell on Amazon.
- ✓ How to create your seller account.
- ✓ How to obtain a bank account in the United States.
- ✓ How Amazon logistics works.
- ✓ How to sell on Amazon without managing inventory.
- ✓ How to find suppliers in China.
- ✓ Techniques to negotiate with your suppliers.
- ✓ How to find the best product.
- ✓ How to advertise your product on Amazon.
- ✓ How to get rich taking advantage of American capitalism.
- ✓ How to use Jungle Scout to find your product.
- ✓ Free tools that will save you time and money.
- ✓ What are the costs of selling on Amazon.
- ✓ How to calculate your earnings and choose the product based on these.

Course content:

- 7 and a half hour of course.
- 8 modules.
- One guide per module.
- Free tools.
- Spreadsheets.
- Real examples.
- You do not need money to start.

You will learn step by step how to create each account, how to use each tool and when you finish the course I guarantee that you will be able to start generating income in Amazon.

You can find more information about our products here:

http://www.how2playmonopoly.com/

Bibliography.

- *The Mistery of Money*, Bernard Lietaer
- *The Death of Banking and Macro Politics*, Hans Schicht
- *100% Money*, Irving Fisher
- *Wall Street, Banks, and American Foreign Policy*, Murray Rothbard
- *A Primer on Money*, Wright Patman
- *Modern Money Mechanics*, Chicago Federal Reserve
- *Debt Cancellation Programs*, G. Edward Griffin
- *The Lost Science of Money*, Stephen Zarlenga
- *The Creature from Jekyll Island*, G. Edward Griffin
- *Money: Whence It Came, Where It Went*, John K. Galbraith
- *The Money Masters: How International Bankers Gained Control of America*, Patrick Carmack, Bill Still.
- *The New World Order*, Jim Cornwell
- *Tragedy and Hope: A History of the World in our Time*, Carroll Quigley
- *The New Depression: The Breakdown of the Paper Money Economy*, Richard Duncan
- *The Dollar Crisis*, Richard Duncan
- *The Purchasing Power of Money: Its Determination and Relation to Credit, Interest and Crises*, Irving Fisher
- *America's Great Depression*, Murray Rothbard
- *The Age of Turbulence*, Alan Greenspan
- *The New Industrial State*, John Kenneth Galbraith
- *Web of Debt*, Ellen Hodgson
- *Tax-Free Wealth*, Tom Wheelwright

- *The Advanced Guide to Real Estate Investing*, Ken McElroy
- *Conspiracy of the Rich*, Robert Kiyosaki
- *Second Chance*, Robert Kiyosaki
- *Collusion: How Central Bankers Rigged The World*, Nomi Prins
- *All The Presidents Bankers*, Nomi Prins
- *Black Tuesday*, Nomi Prins

Contact us

@HowToPlayMonopoly

@Sociedadecaballeros

@ComoJugarMonopolio

howtoplaymonopoly@gmail.com

Web page:

www.how2playmonopoly.com

@HowToPlayMonopoly

Made in the USA
Coppell, TX
15 August 2021

60541832R00189